PETERSON'S

Game Plan for

Getting into

Private

School

Lila Lohr

Peterson's
Thomson Learning™

Australia • Canada • Denmark • Japan • Mexico
New Zealand • Philippines • Puerto Rico • Singapore
Spain • United Kingdom • United States

About Peterson's

Founded in 1966, Peterson's, a division of Thomson Learning, is the nation's largest and most respected provider of lifelong learning online resources, software, reference guides, and books. The Education Supersite[SM] at petersons.com—the Web's most heavily traveled education resource—has searchable databases and interactive tools for contacting U.S.-accredited institutions and programs. CollegeQuest[SM] (CollegeQuest.com) offers a complete solution for every step of the college decision-making process. GradAdvantage[TM] (GradAdvantage.org), developed with Educational Testing Service, is the only electronic admissions service capable of sending official graduate test score reports with a candidate's online application. Peterson's serves over 55 million education consumers annually.

Thomson Learning is among the world's largest providers of lifelong learning information. Headquartered in Stamford, CT, with multiple offices worldwide, Thomson Learning is a division of The Thomson Corporation (TTC), one of the world's leading information companies. TTC operates mainly in the U.S., Canada, and the UK and has annual revenues of over US$6 billion. The Corporation's common shares are traded on the Toronto, Montreal, and London stock exchanges. For more information, visit TTC's Internet address at www.thomcorp. com.

Visit Peterson's Education Center on the Internet (World Wide Web) at www.petersons.com

Library of Congress Cataloging-in-Publication Data

Lohr, Lila.
    Game plan for getting into private school / Lila Lohr.
       p. cm.
    ISBN 0-7689-0387-4
    1. Private schools—United States—Admission. 2. High schools—United States—Admission. I. Title.
LC49.L64 2000
373.12'1—dc21   99-089009
                                                                                                     CIP

Printed in Canada

10 9 8 7 6 5 4 3 2 1

Acknowledgments

Allow me to give special thanks to Diane Rosenberg, our Middle School Head, whose expertise and insight are reflected in this text, and to Wendy Varga, my administrative assistant, who spent hours formatting this project.

Contents

Planning Calendar

Fall/Winter of Seventh Grade

1. Think about what you want in a new school.
2. Talk with your child's teachers about your child's aptitudes and abilities.
3. Think about how you could strengthen your child's candidacy.
4. Collect information from neighbors or friends about schools.
5. Purchase *Peterson's Guide to Private Secondary Schools*.
6. Contact schools and request information.
7. Attend area open houses.

Spring/Summer of Seventh Grade

1. Set up appointments to visit schools/request applications.

Fall of Eighth Grade

1. Attend open houses.
2. Visit schools.
3. Fill out/send in applications on time. Give appropriate forms and envelopes to people writing recommendations.
4. Fill out financial aid applications.

Spring of Eighth Grade

1. Receive acceptance and rejection notifications. Compare financial aid packages.
2. Decide with your child which school is right for your child and your family.

Introduction to Private Schools

If you're picking up this book with some ambivalence, relax, you're in good company. Many families whose children now attend private schools struggled to make that decision. Certainly there are some private school students whose parents, grandparents, and even, great-grandparents attended private schools, but there are many others who never expected to spend their high school years in a private school.

Although there are certainly some excellent public high schools, many families are not happy with the particular public high schools that are available to their children. Overcrowding, concerns about safety, or even a gut feeling that their children aren't being challenged have led many parents to investigate other possibilities. Even the term—*private school*—seems to suggest an exclusiveness that might be appealing to some and be a real turn-off to other children and parents.

My guess is there are a lot of inaccurate stereotypes associated with private schools. Some people would probably describe them as snobby or only for rich kids. Some think that all private school kids are brilliant, while others would assert that all boarding school students have been sent away from broken homes with parents who don't or won't care about their children.

In truth, private schools are different from each other and include a lot of very different students with varied abilities, talents, and backgrounds. Private schools are only similar in their lack of substantial funding or control by the government. The fact that private schools are independent of federal or state control allows them to choose their own students, faculty members, philosophy, and mission. Needless to say different schools have chosen different philosophies and different groups of students to serve.

Of the more than 111,000 schools in this country, less than one quarter are private. Unlike their public school counterparts, private schools receive almost no state or federal support and therefore are not subject to government regulations or controls. Although private schools seem to be springing up monthly, there are only about 26,000 of them across the country. About three quarters are operated by churches or religious organizations. The National Center for Education Statistics reports that there are more Catholic schools than any other religious type. Conservative Christian schools seem to be multiplying quickly, particularly in the southern part of this country.

Clearly some private schools do fit some of the popular stereotypes. Some are incredibly selective and have developed a curriculum and ethos that work best for very bright, talented students. A high percentage of the graduates of these schools go on to the most selective colleges in the country.

Many other private schools include and can be a good fit for students with a range of academic abilities. In fact, contrary to most of the stereotypes, some private schools pride themselves on their ability to help students with different learning issues and styles.

Over the last decade most private schools have worked hard to diversify their student populations. Recognizing the inherent advantages of offering all their students an

There are approximately 26,000 private schools across the United States.

opportunity to know and work with children from diverse backgrounds, many schools have dramatically increased their financial aid pools. This has made it possible for children from all different social and economic strata to come to private schools.

MYTHS AND TRUTHS ABOUT PRIVATE SCHOOLS

Myths	Truths
Only rich families send their children to private school.	Most independent school families would describe themselves as middle-class.
Only brilliant, A+ students go to private schools.	Some schools are very selective, but many seek to serve a range of students.
All private schools are alike.	Private schools vary enormously in size, population, mission and program.
Private school graduates all attend highly competitive colleges and universities.	A very high percentage of private school graduates go on to college, but they attend a wide range of institutions.

Independent Schools

About 25 percent of the country's private schools are nonsectarian. Only about 1,500 of the country's private schools are "independent," meaning they are not affiliated with any state agency or religion. These independent schools include some of the most academically challenging schools in the country. They are governed by an independent Board of Trustees or Directors and are therefore free to make independent decisions about their mission, course of study, students, and faculty members. Most of these independent schools belong to the National Association of Independent Schools (NAIS) and are among the most academically rigorous and well-known private schools in the United States. A good number of them attract students from all around the world. Membership in NAIS requires a school to be nonprofit, nondiscriminatory, and not supported by taxes or church money.

Religious Schools

Many families who want their faith to be taught and reinforced in their child's education choose private Catholic, Protestant, Quaker, or Jewish schools. These schools offer a traditional academic program that is supplemented with courses in religion, often daily or weekly chapel or collection, and a real emphasis on values and morals. Your priest, minister, rabbi, or religious leader can help you find out about any of your local options.

Catholic schools include parochial and diocesan schools, which are managed and controlled by the Catholic Church. Unlike independent religious schools, parochial and diocesan schools usually have a good number of clergy among their teachers. Independent religious schools may be described as affiliated with, for instance, the Episcopal Church, but they are not controlled by that church and have their own elected directors or trustees and few teaching clergy.

For many families, the decision to seek out a private school is motivated by their concern about the lack of any religious training in the public schools. Whether this is a high priority or not, if you are considering a parochial, diocesan, or religiously affiliated school of any type, do your homework carefully. Be sure you know a good deal about the role of religion in each of the schools you are considering because parents have their own convictions about what would be appropriate for their child.

Private schools include day schools, boarding schools, and schools with both boarders and day students. Although the majority of private schools are coed, there are some very fine all-girls or all-boys options to explore. Some private schools are military schools, while others serve students with particular needs or interests. Some are academically demanding and some are designed to help children with various learning styles. Some have national reputations while others are small and only known and appreciated by the families they have served. Many private schools have changed over the years, so it is important to find up-to-date information about their current philosophies and policies.

LOOKING FOR A FIT

Your search for a private school should be about finding a good fit for your child. Just like when you put two pieces of a jigsaw puzzle together, you'll need to look carefully at both pieces of this puzzle; your child and each school.

I have no doubt that right now you know much more about one piece of the puzzle, your child, than you do about various schools that might be a good fit. However, if you're like many of us, it may still be a good idea to take another, more objective look at your child. You need to find a way to think about your child's learning style, natural abilities, untapped aptitudes, and academic maturity and development compared to his peers. Given the love and appreciation parents have of their children, it's sometimes very difficult to see and accept your child's limitations. Holding on to an inflated sense of your child's ability and aptitude will not serve you or your child well. It may result in his applying only to schools beyond his reach, or in an even worse scenario, he may end up being accepted and attending a place that is not a good fit and is quite harmful to his sense of self. We'll try to help you avoid doing that as well as help you to determine what you want your child's school to look like.

Let me be quick to state what seems obvious. This guide is not designed to give you a list of schools to which your child should apply. What we hope to do is help you to look at your child perhaps a bit more objectively. We also have some thoughts about how you might strengthen his candidacy to various schools. We've included some strategies to help you and your child figure out what you want from a private school and some advice about how to learn about and compare various schools. We'll walk you through the application process, providing some insight about visits, interviews, and essays.

We've included some very practical advice about applying for financial aid and have tried to give you some sense of what might help you and your child make a smoother transition to a private school.

The good news is there are a lot of terrific private schools to consider. The bad news is that you and your child will need to commit your time, energy, and thought to this process. I think you'll find, like most families who have done this before you, that it's a very exciting and rewarding experience.

What Private Schools Offer

Chapter 2

For many different reasons, more and more families are looking to private high schools to provide their children with a "better" education. As admission to these schools has become increasingly competitive, parents have been eager to find help with the process. Contrary to the stereotypes, your child does not have to be brilliant, independently wealthy, or the fourth generation of your family to attend a private school.

Many people think of private school children as privileged, jetting off to Switzerland for winter break and the Caribbean for spring vacation. These kids get all As and early acceptance to Yale. They will be CEOs by the age of thirty-five. Certainly children like that do attend private schools, but as you read this guide and learn more about private schools, you will realize that private school children come from a wide range of backgrounds and that many of them experienced the same anxieties you are having about applying to private schools.

Many also assume that the parents of that beautiful, brilliant, Yale-bound child are incredibly rich and write that annual tuition check of $18,000 without a second thought. Tuitions in private schools range from a few thousand dollars to more than $20,000. As you might predict schools in certain areas of the country seem to have consistently charged higher tuitions. For the most part day schools in metropolitan areas like New York, St. Louis,

Washington, San Francisco, and Los Angeles are more expensive than those in rural or even suburban areas.

In 1998–99 in the more than 250 boarding schools that belong to the National Association of Independent Schools (NAIS), the average seven-day boarding tuition for a twelfth grader was $23,400. Yes, some private school parents write tuition checks without blinking an eye, but the majority describe themselves as middle class—and a significant number could not send their children to private schools without substantial financial aid. In 1998–99 16.1 percent of all the students in the NAIS-member schools received some need-based financial aid. In total these students received over $505 million. We'll talk in greater detail in Chapter 6 about the funds that are available and how and when you go about applying for them.

This book will lead you and your family through the process and will provide you with the reasons why other families have chosen private schools. We'll give you some guidance in finding the best match for your child. We'll show you how to learn about private schools, how to develop a shortlist, what to look for when you visit schools, and how to help your child present himself in the best light. We'll dissect and demystify the application process and carefully outline your financial obligations and options.

No, we won't be able to remove all the stress that accompanies such a major decision, but we hope, with our help, you will find this a wonderful opportunity to learn more about your child and find a school where your child will stretch and flourish.

> Many private schools are expensive, but private school families are not all rich. In a few schools more than 25 percent of the students receive need-based financial aid.

WHY PEOPLE ARE CHOOSING PRIVATE SCHOOLS

Private schools all over the country are reporting record increases in applications. In 1998–99, enrollment in NAIS schools alone went up nearly 2 percent to 473,000 students. Some of these applicants are the third or fourth generation in their family to attend these schools and have attended private elementary schools. Their parents have been pleased with the education they have received and feel that the small classes, individual attention, and school's focus on values have helped their children. They are eager to have their children continue in a similar environment. In fact some parents are convinced that because of all the inherent difficulties and dangers of adolescence, it is most important to enroll their children in a private school during their high school years.

Many other applicants are the first in their families to ever even consider leaving their neighborhood public schools. Understandably, many of these families are anxious about the process and whether they are doing the right thing. They feel disloyal and concerned that even if their children are fortunate enough to be accepted, they may end up hating the new school and never feel like they belong there.

Academic Rigor

Sadly, the dramatically increased number of applications to private schools reflects a growing dissatisfaction with public schools. NAIS recently reported the results of a national opinion poll on people's perceptions of independent schools. It indicated that the public associates the following words with private schools:

- Safe

- Selective

- Personalized

- Caring

Many feel their children are not being challenged enough in public schools. Some of these children are doing well but clearly could do more, could be stretched intellectually. From their parents' point of view, they spend far too much time watching television, wandering around the mall, or playing games on their computers. Parents are worried that they neither write very well nor are very aware of what's going on in the world. They have friends with children in private schools who seem to be doing much more advanced work than their public school peers. Some feel their children are actively bored and are no longer motivated or engaged. Parents may have difficulty articulating the specifics, but for lack of a better description, they're in search of a school that is more academically rigorous—parents want something "better" for their children.

Some parents think that academic rigor will come with smaller classes, more personal attention, and teachers who will nurture and promote each child's talents. Although the numbers vary, there is no question that private schools offer smaller classes than most public schools in the country. According to the National Center for Education Statistics, in 1998–99 the median student-teacher ratio in NAIS schools was 9 to 1 while that in public schools was 17 to 1. Many families would be happy to have their children in an average class of 17 students, but unfortunately many public schools have classes of over 30 students.

Smaller classes also make it difficult for a student to hide or slide. In a room with only 14 other students, it is difficult to remain uninvolved or consistently unprepared. Teachers can get to know 15 students much better and faster than 30. Smaller classes promote more faculty member–student interaction, and most kids benefit from and respond to teachers who know and care about them.

As in many colleges, the courses that private schools require all ninth, tenth, or eleventh grade students to take tend to meet in larger sections, while the electives and advanced level courses often have only a handful of students. Given the traditional private school emphasis on teaching writing, you will often find that English classes are quite small. It is also not unusual to find English teachers spending hours outside of class working with one or two students on their writing. Many schools schedule regular tutorial meetings to allow an individual child to benefit from this personal focus. This out-of-class, individual support is something to take note of as you visit schools. For some students this one-on-one work is where their most significant learning takes place. Not all private schools have the luxury of providing this type of support, but most pride themselves on the accessibility of their faculty members.

Parents looking for smaller classes are also drawn to the adviser systems that characterize most private schools. Although the specifics vary from school to school, most private schools find many ways to promote close student–teacher relationships. These connections are possible

> Families turn to private schools in search of academic rigor, smaller classes, and an emphasis on values. Others are erroneously convinced that with their child's acceptance letter to a private school they have secured a ticket to the most competitive colleges in the country.

because, in addition to smaller classes, each teacher only advises, or acts as a counselor, to a small number of students. Most teachers also coach or direct extracurricular activities that allow them other opportunities outside of class to interact with their students.

The Arts

Families who have seen significant cutbacks in their public schools are eager to find schools that will provide extensive opportunities in the arts. Some private schools offer a remarkable menu of art courses for their students. Almost all require at least one taste of the arts, whether that be in the form of a mixed-media course or a choice of specific electives. Larger schools and those with a special emphasis on the arts often offer courses that used to be available only at the collegiate level. For many students, this opportunity to express themselves, whether in painting, in music composition, or on the stage, is central to their sense of self and becomes the defining piece of their high school experience.

Extracurricular Activities

Although there is a wide range of programs in private schools—depending primarily on their resources and philosophy—most schools recognize the importance of providing an extended menu of extracurricular choices for their students. Many private high school students participate in several different clubs and play several sports. In some of the smaller schools, even fairly modest athletes can enjoy playing on several school teams. It's interesting to note that a recent NAIS report on public perception of independent schools suggests that many people do not realize how many activities and sports are available at the majority of private schools. Certainly a small day school, especially in a rural area, will not be able to offer the range of activities that a large public high school will, but some of the larger day and boarding schools offer activity menus that rival small colleges.

In truth, it's important to remember that given the academic demands of most private schools, your child will only be able to take advantage of a finite number of clubs and activities each year.

Values and Character

Other families are drawn to private schools because of their greater emphasis on values, character, and standards. Removed from issues such as separation of church and state, private schools seek out opportunities to talk with their students about their morals and values. Rather than shy away from these conversations, faculty members find them invigorating and a wonderful way to engage adolescents. Although some private schools have clear religious affiliations, almost all address issues of integrity, service to one's community, and morality openly and repeatedly.

In recent years, many private schools have developed a community service requirement for graduation.

In recent years, many private schools have developed a community service requirement for graduation. Many students go well beyond these requirements and spend an enormous amount of time volunteering in soup kitchens, organizing walk-a-thons for different charities, and working with less fortunate children. For some students these are the most significant experiences of their high school years. They certainly provide an important opportunity for kids to look beyond themselves and to question the status quo. Often idealistic and critical, it's not surprising that adolescents are drawn to helping society's underdogs and the needy.

Many of these same parents who are looking for an emphasis on values recognize the power of adolescent peers and want their children to go to a school where it's okay to be smart, where it's the norm to do your homework every night, and where you're expected to go to college. Private schools have the freedom to not admit or expel students who are disruptive or unwilling to abide by a school's rules. Unlike some public schools that end up promoting almost every student to the next grade, private schools feel free to require students to attend summer school, repeat a grade, or leave the school if they don't meet their academic or behavioral requirements.

Security

Certainly, the extensive media attention given to the recent incidents of school violence has heightened parental concern about school safety. All parents want their children to be safe; the NAIS Public Opinion Poll reported that better than half of respondents agreed that "structured" and "safe" were appropriate descriptions of independent schools. Although private school administrators recognize that they can't guarantee anything, they do hope that their ability to provide extensive individual attention to each student will create a safe, secure community. In the past few years, even private schools have focused more attention and resources on campus security. Security cards, pass card systems, alarms, and visitor badges are now commonplace on campuses, whereas a decade ago people came and went at will. Although many schools have attempted to make their schools less accessible to anyone who wants to wander in, most independent school heads would argue that their best defense against campus violence lies in the fact that each student and each adult is well known to at least several teachers and/or administrators.

Community

As you begin to research individual schools, you'll probably read a lot about community. Private schools, large and small, work hard to create a partnership with their parents and a sense of community for all their constituents. While recognizing that high school students relish a certain degree of autonomy and independence, parents are encouraged to take an active role in a day school. Children clearly benefit when their parents and teachers trust, respect, and communicate regularly with each other, so teachers are urged to develop open, candid relationships with parents.

Obviously, it is more difficult for parents of boarders to be physically involved in their school, but boarding schools encourage open and regular dialogue that both respects a child's privacy and desire for independence and provides appropriate support and limits. Unlike many public schools, where students and faculty members can only be in the buildings during strictly prescribed hours, you'll visit many private day schools where teachers and students come early in the morning and stay late into the evening. In fact, many of these high school students view their school as their home.

Boarding schools feel a tremendous responsibility to provide a homelike community for their students, for whom the school is home nine months of the year. Dorm parents

Boarding schools feel a tremendous responsibility to provide a home-like sense of community for their students for whom the school is home nine months of the year.

play a critical role in overseeing and shaping the lives of their students. Many parents marvel at the faculty's willingness to be available to students almost 24 hours a day. Dorm parents make chocolate chip cookies with their students, listen to their concerns, and help them sort through both academic and personal problems. Dorm parents often have their own children living with them, which contributes to the home-life ambiance. Many students enjoy babysitting and interacting with these younger children.

Ticket to the Ivy League

Some parents seek out a private school because they believe it will be their child's ticket to a competitive college. This is tricky ground because the college admissions process is not that simple.

Going to a private school these days does not guarantee admission to any college, much less the most competitive ones. A few generations ago, schools like Andover, St. Albans, and Gilman could call up colleges like Princeton and say, "We'll be sending you 16 boys next year." Strong all-girl schools like Westover, Miss Fine's, and Brearley had similar relationships with Vassar, Smith, and Wellesley. But those days are over.

Today, the most competitive colleges are eager to diversify their classes, and they accept many more talented students from public schools than from private schools. A fairly small percentage of the most heavily recruited high school athletes come from private schools. Many well-known, strong private schools are experiencing increased pressure from parents who can't understand why the school is no longer sending 25 percent of their students to the Ivy

League. As the cost of a private school has steadily increased, parents become even angrier when their $24,000-a-year tuition does not lead to an acceptance to Yale.

It is important to note that private schools can offer much more personalized college counseling. Counselors advise a smaller number of students whom they know well and to who they can offer advice about where to apply and how to present themselves. These counselors spend hours talking with each child about what courses to take and what activities to pursue both at school and during the summer. Teacher recommendations reflect the close personal connections between students and faculty members and can therefore be persuasive. Clearly teachers who know their students well are able to cite specific examples of their work and evidence of their aptitude. This kind of individual, personal guidance is simply not possible when one college counselor works with hundreds of students. One can also argue that the traditional private school emphasis on reading and writing, the rigorous academic standards, and the ability to focus on each student's individual learning style allow them to graduate students who are both attractive candidates to colleges and who are prepared to cope with college work. Some college admissions offices have had a long tradition of working with candidates from a particular private school. They know the school well and know that the students will be prepared.

Not every child, including some extremely talented ones, belongs at Stanford or Duke. Effective college counselors need to know a great deal about a good many schools if they are going to be able to direct each student to the appropriate colleges. Good college counseling has to do with finding a good fit between a student and college. In the same way, searching for a private school shouldn't be about finding the best school but should focus on finding a good fit for your child.

A GOOD FIT

So how do you find a good fit for your child? You need to spend some time thinking about who your child is and who she could become. Although most of us find it difficult to be objective about our children, looking for a new school can be a great opportunity to talk to your children about their strengths, interests, and aspirations. Some kids and parents have enjoyed making lists of what the child does well, what she likes and doesn't like about herself, and what she hopes to do in college and beyond.

Getting A Good Look At Your Child

How do you find a good fit for your child? Start by spending some time thinking about who your child is and who she could become.

Explore your child's likes and dislikes. Does he like to spend time alone? Does he like being with younger children? Is it important to him to spend a lot of time outside? Who is his favorite teacher and why? What does he think about wearing a uniform to school? Does he like making choices, or would he rather be given a list of things to do? Is he excited about meeting lots of new people, or does he like being in a smaller group or a smaller school? What's his favorite place and why? Does the weather matter much to him?

These are wonderful conversations that our busy lives don't always allow. Not all parents and children embrace them with the same enthusiasm, but for some they pave the way to creating lists of things to look for when you visit and compare different schools. We'll spend more time talking about these lists as we prepare for our school visits in Chapter 4.

As you struggle to flesh out an objective view of your child, her teachers and other adult friends could be helpful. Asking her Little League coach, piano teacher, scout leader, or uncle how they see your daughter could give you some new insights into her strengths, her learning style, and her interests. It might be productive to ask them to describe the kind of school where they think your daughter would flourish. They might even suggest specific schools.

Your Child's Academic Aptitude and Performance

It's also important to have an objective evaluation of your child's academic aptitude and performance. Reviewing your child's report cards and standardized tests with her teacher is an important part of finding the right fit in a new school. You need some sense of her ability and performance relative to her own class and to a larger community (either local or national). Begin by finding out how your daughter compares to her classmates. Talk with her teacher and ask him for some assessment relative to the class. Experienced elementary school teachers can usually offer valuable insight into your child's ability and performance. Is she working hard, or does she earn her grades with a minimum of effort? Despite a teacher's understandable and appropriate reluctance to discuss the aptitude and performance of other individual students, he'll usually be willing to give you some sense of how your child compares to her classmates in terms of ability, effort, and performance. This will help in your search for an appropriate school.

Standardized Tests

Although some children do well in school but not well on standardized tests, these exams provide valuable comparative data. Your son's sixth grade teacher may give mostly Bs, and it is difficult to know what that means relative to children in other sixth grade classrooms. Almost all private schools require some sort of standardized test as part of the admissions process. We'll talk more in Chapter 3 about how to help your child prepare.

While you hope to have a realistic view of your child's ability, this is an important ingredient of a successful school search. Unfortunately some teachers shy away from being completely candid with parents about their child's potential and performance. If you feel there is some inconsistency between your child's report card and his standardized tests, be sure to pursue this with his teachers. Widespread grade inflation has misled some parents and children as to their abilities relative to their peers.

For some families this attempt to develop a clearer sense of their child's abilities has led to an individual assessment by a learning specialist. These evaluations are expensive, but they can provide insight into unusual learning styles and/or learning gaps. If the information is presented in a constructive way, every child can benefit enormously from understanding his own strengths and weaknesses. Realizing how he learns best and what he needs to do to compensate for his weaknesses can be very helpful. You hear many adults comment that to remember something, they need to write it down. This self-awareness could be helpful to a seventh grader as well.

Some parents are reluctant to share this information with their child's current teachers and/or the schools to which he is applying, but I have rarely seen this work to the child's advantage. On occasions when parents have not shared this information, a school will admit a child who might not have been accepted had the complete picture been known. Unfortunately this is not discovered until later, when the child is struggling and miserable. It would seem that his parents focused on getting their child into the best or most prestigious school rather than one where he had the best chance to succeed and thrive.

Remember that most schools don't accept kids with certain test scores just so they can brag about how high their average test scores are, but rather because they have found that kids with these scores have the best chance of being successful in their school. Their experience has usually shown (although there are always some exceptions) that kids need to have performed at that level on standardized tests to be able to handle the school's requirements. Every school wants to accept kids who will do well and thrive.

> **Remember that most schools accept kids with certain test scores because they have found that kids with these scores have the best chance of succeeding in their school.**

Some parents can become disappointed and surprised to learn that their child's standardized tests are not terribly strong. Low test scores do not mean a child cannot go to a private school, but they suggest that you should focus on a particular set of schools where your child has a good chance of being admitted and of finding success. Although it may be appropriate to encourage students to apply to some reach schools (where they may not have a great chance of being accepted), it's also important to have children apply to schools where the odds are good that they *will* be successful. To find that group of schools you need to have a good sense of your child's academic potential and performance.

Location

To find that group of schools that fit, you also need to establish your geographic boundaries. Are you considering boarding schools, and if so, can they be anywhere in the country? Some families have limited their search to no more than a 4-hour car ride away. Others have wanted their children to see a different part of the country or be near other members of the family. The cost of transportation to and from school has been an important part of some family decisions. Other families who have chosen to go the boarding school route are in search of the best fit for their child, so the location is almost immaterial.

As boarding schools spend more time and attention providing weekend activities for their students, I think it's worth talking about how your boarding-school child might want to spend his weekends. If urban life and its many possibilities appeal to him, I would keep that in mind as you research schools. Although all boarding schools provide some special weekends, most activities will take place no further than an hour away from the school. Obviously these will vary tremendously if the school is in the middle of a big city or in rural countryside.

Are you, like more and more families today, willing and able to relocate to send your child to a specific school? A California family decided they wanted their children to go to school on the East Coast. They researched schools all over the region, chose one in the Princeton area, and moved nearby. This may seem like an extreme example, so if you feel that desperate about your child's school options near your home, you should consider a boarding school instead of relocating the entire family.

Most families who are not considering boarding schools are looking to find the best school for their children within a limited geographic area. Typically a parent is transferred to a city like Atlanta and is trying to find the best school there. When a family is looking for a private school because they're relocating, they will often not purchase a new home until they have chosen a school.

Probably the largest number of private school applicants come from families who are leaving public schools but staying in the same area. With the exception of those who live in major metropolitan areas, they choose from a fairly short list of private schools.

Boarding Schools

Although the stereotype of a boarding school describes it as a place for children from dysfunctional families, in reality, many talented, happy, well-adjusted students choose to go away to school. In 1998–99 NAIS schools had over 43,000 boarders, close to 25 percent of whom were international students. A 1997 report by the Association of Boarding Schools indicated that the greatest number of these boarding students in American schools came from South Korea, Japan, Mexico, and Saudi Arabia.

In 1998–99 NAIS schools had over 43,000 boarders, close to 25 percent of whom were international students.

Many boarding school applicants come from families with a tradition of going away to school. These parents are appreciative of the opportunities they had to study and live with students from all over the country and abroad. They know firsthand about the extensive range of extracurricular opportunities, the sense of independence, the pleasure of living with peers, and the sense of belonging to a community that boarding schools can provide. For them, their boarding school had a much greater impact on their lives than their colleges. They attend their reunions faithfully and are still in close touch with their boarding school friends.

Other families have had neither boarding nor day school experience, but they do not wish to relocate and their town doesn't have any high schools that seem right for their children. They are looking at boarding schools for the same reasons other families have switched from public schools to private day schools: smaller classes, academic rigor, and individual attention. They may also know of the loyalty of most boarding school graduates to their schools, which speaks volumes about their remarkable sense of connection to the school. For three or four years, it was home.

Many parents have strong feelings about whether they want their children to go to boarding school. For some, where both parents travel a great deal, other siblings demand extra attention, an only child seems lonely, or the local peer group seems troublesome, boarding school seems like a godsend. Others fear that if they allow their kids to go away to school, they won't be a part of their child's day-to-day high school experience. These parents are often concerned that boarding school peers will have too strong an influence or that they will lose touch with their child.

Some families have been thrilled to find a third alternative, a five-day boarding plan, where students go home Friday afternoon. A few schools offer only this boarding option, while other schools include day students, five-day boarders, and seven-day boarders. Transportation options and expenses will be important considerations as well as finding out whether the current five-day boarders feel that they really belong at the school.

If the weekend activities are too inviting and central to the school's experience, day students may feel marginalized. In some schools where this has occurred, the school has made it possible for day students to board on special occasions. In other schools, Friday afternoons are really tough for the boarders as they watch their classmates head home for the weekend.

In any combination of day, five-day boarding, and seven-day boarding students, the numbers will be important. No one, especially adolescents, wants to feel like everyone else is doing something fun. Your child may not enjoy being in the minority. Most successful combinations include enough of each group for all kids to feel like they are part of the school.

Some parents and children have been pleased with the experience of being a day student in a boarding school. Assuming that there are enough day students to feel like they are a part of the school, this situation can give your child an opportunity to experience many of the advantages of a boarding school without leaving home.

Going to school with students from all over the country, if not the world, will appeal to many kids, as will the opportunity to participate in a host of weekend and evening activities. Some schools find it necessary to limit the participation of their day students, and still others find it challenging to integrate the two populations. These schools usually work hard to create "one school," encouraging the day students to invite the boarders home for weekends, setting up local "host" families for each interested boarder, and finding ways to attract day students to weekend activities.

> The five-day boarding plan, where students live at school during the week and go home Friday afternoon, is a popular alternative to seven-day boarding programs.

These are personal issues. There is no correct answer. Some children thrive in boarding school. For others it's not the best fit. Talking with other children and parents about how and why they chose to go to a boarding or a day school might help you and your child clarify your thinking. Some adolescents prefer the required study hall to nightly arguments with their parents about homework. Others bristle at the thought of dictated lights out and restrictions on leaving campus. Some relish the idea of constant company while others dread the lack of privacy. Some are excited about the prospect of living with kids from all over the world, while others worry that the dorms will seem too big, too impersonal, too foreign. Visiting and talking with current students are the best ways to separate fact from fiction.

Although there are some circumstances that might make it advisable to send a child away to school against his wishes, in most cases the school and child will only be a good fit if the child wants to go there. Some parents feel that choosing a school is up to them and that their children should have little, if any, input. Others recognize that in a best-case scenario, child and parents would conduct a joint search and come to the same conclusions.

Many families have found a middle ground. The parents and child have worked through the search process together, coming up with a list of schools to which the child will apply. They might not agree on which should be the first choice, but they can live with the child going to any one of them.

I think parents need to decide in the beginning how much choice they're comfortable giving their child, but I also think it's unfair to let a child apply to a school that you have no intention of sending her to. If the school is unacceptable to the parent, the child shouldn't apply there. Although more and more children are being allowed to make more decisions and choices about what they do and with whom, the choice of a high school—private or public—is a important decision with lifelong implications. It's a decision with serious financial implications and one that should be made based on a careful consideration of the many factors that will make a particular school a good fit for a particular child.

Unfortunately, but understandably, many eighth and ninth grade applicants can be influenced by a host of impressions that don't really reveal a school's character. In Chapter 4 we will talk at length about what to look for when you visit schools, but even with that guidance, I think it's appropriate that parents have a strong voice in framing the shortlist. This is too important and expensive a decision to be based on the cute tour guide, the number of dogs on campus, and the delicious lunch. I'm not suggesting that these things don't matter, but rather that they should not be allowed to lead your child to apply to a school that you know is not a good fit or will not provide the things that sent you in search of a private school.

If, after some research and a visit, a school feels wrong for your child, don't ignore your instincts.

While there is much homework you can do to help you and your child make a good, informed decision, you don't want to ignore your basic instincts. If, after some research and a visit, a school feels wrong for your child, don't ignore your instincts. If you've given careful thought to what you're looking for in a school for this child, don't get sidetracked. It may be appropriate for an eighth or ninth grader to help choose from among a list of schools that are acceptable to her parents, but most kids simply don't know enough—nor are they willing or able to learn enough—to be given carte blanche in the search for a private high school.

Single-Sex Schools

Although many single-sex private schools went coed in the late 1960s and early 1970s, recent research and conversation about the advantages of single-sex schools, particularly those for girls, seems to have fueled an increased interest in this option. Of the 1,025 NAIS schools, 91 (8.9 percent) are girls' schools and 76 (7.4 percent) are boys' schools. Specific information is available from the National Coalition of Girls' Schools and the International Boys School Coalition.

Graduates of single-sex schools will argue compellingly that this kind of environment allowed them to concentrate more on their academics, develop more confidence, find and strengthen their own voices, and be taught by teachers who wanted to work exclusively with them. Current students in single-sex schools appreciate the opportunities for leadership and report feeling more comfortable "being themselves" without having to play to an audience of the other sex. Single-sex schools today work hard to provide numerous opportunities for students to interact with boys and girls from other schools. They recognize the need to convince prospective students that they wouldn't be coming to a monastery or nunnery. Many prospective parents recognize the inherent advantages of a single-sex school, although their children may need to be convinced. Often parents are not sure if they want to send their child to a single-sex school, but as they make mental lists of what they are looking for, the appeal of a single-sex school becomes clearer.

Boys' Schools

Parents of boys, especially single mothers and families where both parents work long hours, are often eager to find a school that will recognize their sons' tremendous physical energy as well as provide them with critical male role models. Close relationships with men who teach and coach boys can be an extremely powerful part of both a boarding and day school experience.

Needless to say, not all boys respond to the same role models, so it's important to look at the different teachers in any school you consider. Most boys will benefit from being in an environment where they are shown that there are many ways to be successful men—as coaches, artists, musicians, teachers, or writers, to name a few.

Girls' Schools

Many parents of girls recognize the advantages of an all-girls' school, but they are hesitant about their ability to convince their daughters to consider this option. Some girls thrive in coed middle schools, while others seem to lose their confidence and their voices. Just as some girls are comfortable and confident dealing with boys, others are desperately in need of female companionship.

Each girl is different, although most will thrive in either a coed or a girls' school. Each school is also unique, so while a particular all-girls' school may be perfect for

> Although their numbers declined dramatically in the 1970s and 1980s, single-sex schools have experienced an increase in applications. This may be related to recent research and attention to the different ways boys and girls learn and need to be nurtured.

your daughter, another might not be a good fit. Your oldest child might excel at the local private day school, but for your youngest, it could be a disaster. At the risk of banging the same old drum, you need to look for a school that will best fit this particular child. Many parents seem to forget this when it comes to choosing a school for their second or third child. Although it certainly may be easier to have all your children in the same school, it's important to find one that is a good match for each child. That may not always be the same school.

Gender Issues in Coed Schools

Articles and books by authors such as Carol Gilligan and Mary Pfeifer have popularized the notion that many girls would be better off in all-girl classes or schools. And respected school psychologists like Michael Thompson have pointed out the many ways in which schools do not encourage or tolerate the best psychological development of boys.

It's interesting to note the response to these findings within coeducational schools, where teachers and administrators are struggling to support and enhance the development of both girls and boys. It's a challenge to create an environment in which girls are encouraged to speak out more and reap the benefits of competition and team work while boys are simultaneously encouraged to work collaboratively and to experience a full range of emotional responses.

How schools choose to address these gender issues is something to consider when you visit schools and peruse their literature. Many formerly all-boy schools that are now coed have worked hard to create an environment that is equally responsive to the needs of girls. It may be of interest to look at the percentages of girls and boys enrolled, the number of leadership positions that are held by each, and the number of athletic teams for girls and boys. Although more women traditionally teach at the elementary level in private coed schools and in high schools, you might want to look at the faculty gender mix, particularly in a coed school that only recently changed from single-sex. Some parents are concerned about the all-male leadership in many coed schools. It's clearly important that there be a variety of good role models, male and female, for boys and girls. We'll talk a little more about this in Chapter 4 when we prepare for your visits.

In an ideal search you and your child would stay open-minded about single-sex schools. Some kids absolutely refuse to consider them, while others are pleasantly surprised when they visit vibrant, exciting single-sex campuses that include lots of opportunities to meet boys or girls from other schools. Forcing a child to attend a single-sex school when he or she is absolutely adamant about not going is a risky decision that can have disastrous results. Certainly there may be unusual circumstances that make it necessary. We all know students who have reluctantly gone to a school or college and ended up loving it. It may be helpful to ask the school to provide you with the names of some other initially reluctant but currently happy students.

"Ivy League Syndrome"

As you begin exploring and reading, you'll quickly realize that there is a wide range of private schools, each with its own emphasis, strengths, and personality. Although some children belong in and will flourish in the nationally known academic powerhouses that have graduated generations of successful leaders, many others do not. It is critical that you avoid what I call the "Ivy League Syndrome." Sufferers are convinced that the seven colleges that make up the Ivy League are the best colleges in the country and that anyone who doesn't go to one of them is getting an inferior education. Some students can only come into their own when they are surrounded by equally talented kids. But just as there are many excellent colleges and universities, there are many excellent private schools—it is most important that you find the right fit for your child.

Just as there are many excellent colleges and universities, there are many excellent private schools—it is most important that you find the right fit for your child.

You want to find a school where she will be challenged and stretched but where she will also feel she belongs and is successful. It's important when you consider each school that you find out what it takes to be successful there. Is the school demanding enough to challenge your child? Is it also sufficiently supportive and responsive to her strengths and learning style to make her feel good about herself and her accomplishments?

Some private schools seem less clear about who they serve best and what it takes to be successful there. Others are crystal clear. Contrary to some generalizations about private schools, not all are designed to educate bright, well-adjusted, well-rounded children. Some have tailored their programs to met the needs of special children, such as outstanding skiers, gifted musicians, kids who have encountered academic and social difficulties in other schools, or computer whizzes. To find a school that will best meet your child's needs, you need to be clear about those needs and how each school would go about meeting those needs.

Avoiding Early Specialization

What makes this even more elusive is that every child is, and should be, multidimensional. Most are interested in several different things and should be encouraged to embrace various possibilities. I see so many high school and college students who mapped out their entire life by age 12. This early one-dimensional focus can preclude considering lots of terrific options.

In a world where few college athletes can play more than one sport, it's not surprising that we see more and more younger children playing one sport all year. No doubt inspired by the possibility of their child earning a college scholarship or at the least improving his chance of acceptance at a competitive school, parents are encouraging kids to specialize at a young age.

While there are gifted athletes or musicians for whom year-round pursuit of one sport or one musical instrument might make sense, most children will not perform at the Metropolitan Opera or play on a World Cup soccer team. Children do learn a lot from focusing their energy on one activity and mastering a specific set of skills, but parents need to think carefully about this. I know a boy who was the number-one 12-year-old tennis player in his state. Three years later he quit playing competitively. He had simply burned out and had missed out on a lot of traditional boyhood experiences. Another student, a talented skier, chose a school that put downhill racing first and academics second. She eventually stopped skiing, but she also realized she wasn't prepared to go to college. She had assumed that her passion for skiing would continue to consume her and would drive her college choice and career.

Kids and parents need to be careful when they consider the academic equivalent of early specialization. You hear young children announce that they're going to be actors or doctors or investment bankers. It's great to see that kind of enthusiasm and focus, but it can also be counterproductive if it's allowed to drive too many decisions. Psychology, sociology, and filmmaking resonate with students who can be weary of the basics—biology, math, physics, and history. Electives are superb and attractive compliments to a traditional curriculum, and advisers are quick to point out the advantages of taking a balanced academic program, even for children who are focused on one interest or career path.

As you learn about individual schools, it is important to compare the curricular offerings, including what courses each school requires of all its students. We'll talk more about reviewing school materials in Chapter 3.

YOUR CHILD'S HESITATION

It is important to understand that many children who will eventually be happy and successful in a private school are initially hesitant about making the change. They are worried that everyone else there will be smarter, richer, and more popular and that they won't be able to do the work, they won't make new friends, and their old friends will resent and drop them.

These are heavy-duty worries for seventh and eighth graders. Acknowledging these fears and talking about them is an important first step. All of us harbor some anxiety about major changes in our lives. It's helpful to tell your child that this is normal and understandable. Have him talk with older children who have weathered the transition successfully. Visit schools so he will see that not everyone looks like the extremely attractive, gleefully happy children featured in the school's literature. Sit in on classes to give him an opportunity to see the type of work the kids are actually doing as opposed to the sometimes intimidating descriptions in the school catalogs. It may be that you visit a school where there is an enormous gap between the work your child has been doing and what would be expected of him in this new setting. This can be unnerving to your child, but it is also an opportunity to talk with the admissions officers about their expectations and how they support new students. We'll talk some more about these potentially surprising school visits in Chapter 4.

This understandable fear of not measuring up, either academically or socially, may take a while to fade. Many students have spent at least the first semester in their new private schools feeling rather lonely and isolated. It may be hard to make new friends, and they may find themselves surrounded by the kids who are "richer" or "smarter" or "more beautiful." But with time, most new kids find others with whom they feel more comfortable.

Some of these transitions seem easier when there are a lot of new kids. Transferring to a private high school in ninth grade, even in a kindergarten through grade 12 school, usually means there will be more new kids than in tenth or eleventh grades. Joining a K–12 day school in high school can be more difficult if most of the kids have been there together for several years.

> Be prepared—many children get cold feet about actually going to a private school. They worry that they aren't smart enough or that they'll lose their old friends and won't make new ones.

Sometimes your child's worries about his current friends are well placed. Some of the neighborhood kids and their parents will resent your decision to leave the local school. They see your departure as critical of the school, and, therefore, critical of them. They may wonder why the school isn't good enough for you or your child if it's good enough for them. And for some families, it's particularly difficult because they would also love to leave.

Talking about your decision in a way that emphasizes your child's needs rather than the current school's faults may help. Obviously you're not going to make anyone feel better by pointing out all the things wrong with the neighborhood school and all the ways the new school will be better. It's easier for others to listen to why you think your son needs to be in a smaller class where the teacher can make sure he pays attention than to hear you rant about how his current class is huge and the teacher doesn't pay attention to him. Making a concerted effort to keep in touch with and reach out to the neighborhood kids and their parents may ease the transition.

Many children do eventually lose touch with their old friends as they become more and more integrated into their new schools. For some, living in two worlds can be difficult. They may be ridiculed by their neighborhood friends for wearing a uniform or resented for going to the school with the "rich" kids. The neighborhood friends may have much more free time and won't understand why your child spends so much time at school and doing his homework. They might accuse him of being a snob and disinterested in their old past times. He may simply have too much homework to hang around the way he used to. His new friends may dress and talk differently than his neighborhood friends. Some children do manage to have close friends in both worlds and actually blend the two. But many find this balancing act too exhausting and eventually spend less and less time with their old pals.

NOT ALL CHILDREN SHOULD GO

One final caveat as you begin your search: Just as not all high school graduates belong at Stanford and not all talented ninth graders will flourish at the most competitive day schools, not all children will flourish in private schools. I've touched on some of those reasons, and certainly there are others.

- Some children are not able or willing to meet the rigorous academic standards.

- Some children do not want to straddle the two disparate worlds of home and school.

- Some children do not feel private school is worth giving up the pluses of a neighborhood school.

- Some children feel they do not belong in a new school.

These are exceptions, but they do happen and are worth keeping in mind as you struggle to focus on your objective view of your child and how well she will fit into the schools you're considering. It's also important to remember that if, in fact, you choose a school that does not seem to be a good fit, this is not a life sentence. Just as some college students transfer from one college to another, a few kids may need to change high schools. As overwhelming and exhausting as that might sound, it's not the end of the world—it can be managed.

That said, we're going to do everything we can to help you find a good spot, but we have lots of homework to do first. Let's get started.

Starting Your Search

Chapter 3

If you think you want your child to enter a private high school in ninth grade, you need to begin your own serious research while she's in seventh grade. You'll have no doubt heard comments about various schools along the way from neighbors or friends. It's time to start ferreting out that information and collecting it in some systematic way. Although some students switch schools in tenth and eleventh grade, it may be easier to go to a new school in ninth grade. Your child will receive the benefits of the full four years, and it's easier to be new with a large group of other new students.

It's important to decide why you're looking for a new school and what you hope that school will provide for your child. Some parents enjoy making a list of the specific attributes they want in a new school. Others want to explore all options, confident that there must be something better. Although some parents choose not to involve their children in the initial explorations, I think it's advisable to let your child know that you are considering a change and are going to try to find out more about the options.

Children who are quite happy in their current school or who are looking forward to going to the local high school with their friends might be resistant to this possibility. Unless you have made a definitive decision, assure your child that you are only in an exploratory mode and that she will be part of the discussion and decision-making process. Explain why you think a change is worth considering. As

Game Plan for Getting into Private School

you explore the options and see what possibilities are within your child's reach, it will become more clear as to whether you feel it is mandatory or only mildly preferable for your child to go to a private school. It's important to sort this out because it should guide you in your interactions with your child.

As you learn more about your child's academic profile and the various schools that might be options, you will also be able to compare and contrast them with the public school options. You may be fortunate to have some strong public high schools that, upon close inspection, don't seem dramatically different from the available private schools. In that case, and particularly if your child is not interested in going to a private school, you might choose not to fight that battle.

For many families, studying private schools convinces them that a public school education is not what they're looking for. As they learn more, they feel more and more strongly that their child belongs in a private school. As parents, you need to decide if this is the right decision, no matter what your child's initial reaction. It is often difficult for a seventh or eighth grader to see the big picture and understand what a different school could mean for him.

MODELING DECISION MAKING

The search for a new school is a wonderful opportunity to show your child how to make a difficult decision. For some reason, most adolescents think adults make arbitrary, snap decisions (Be home at 10:30; No, you can't spend Friday and Saturday night at Susie's, etc.) or that adults just know what to do. It's important for our children to see us take the time, do the homework, get input from others, weigh the pros and cons, and then make a decision. This is a great chance for them to learn that there are trade-offs and compromises in any decision and that it's important to try to identify those trade-offs early in the process. Most schools will have appealing and disappointing features. There is no such thing as a perfect school. One may have a great academic program but seem too big. Another may be in a perfect location but seem too strict and a bit out of touch. Another may have a strong athletic program but limited opportunities in the arts.

The search for a private high school requires much more parental involvement and direction because seventh and eighth graders do not have the time, resources, or perspective to ferret out a list of appropriate options. Given that most children will be conducting a similar search for a college in three or four years, this is an ideal time to prepare them for that process. By the time they are juniors and seniors in high school, they will be better prepared to take the lead in conducting a college search.

Kids who are nervous about the private school admission process often leap at one school just to get it over with.

This may help you and your child avoid the sometimes disastrous, premature decision that School B is the only school for you. Although School B may, in fact, belong on your shortlist, you need to help establish some acceptable options should this not work. Kids who are nervous about the process often leap at one school just to get the process over. They often also have a harder time assessing their academic strengths and chances of being accepted and successful at different schools. They will need parental help. Setting up a calendar, collecting data in an organized fashion, soliciting information from many sources, recognizing the importance of meeting deadlines, and talking about how best to present yourself are all lifetime skills that will be useful to your children.

Openly acknowledging that you're trying to show them how to go about making a good decision will probably make you more mindful of your own behavior. It often keeps you on your toes when you know someone is watching your every step. Some kids may enjoy the details of collecting information and setting up appointments, but most will focus more on the picture catalogs and what they've heard about the schools from their friends. Parents need to be sure that this information gathering process is sufficiently objective and extensive enough to give them an accurate snapshot of several schools.

Although it seems helpful and fair to alert your child to your concerns about her present school and your interest in finding an appropriate private school, I think it's important to avoid fixating on the change. I've seen children stop working, stop making an effort, and become marginalized in their current school because they become so focused on going to a new school.

You want your child to continue to work hard, do well, and make the most of her current situation. Not only will those behaviors make for a better year, they will also improve her chances of being accepted at a private school.

LEARNING ABOUT PRIVATE SCHOOLS

It's important to realize that the school your uncle attended is probably not the same school today. Even the most prestigious, well known private schools have changed in the last ten or fifteen years. Talking with other private school children and their parents will provide you with firsthand information.

If you don't know any private school families, your pediatrician, Little League coach, minister, or scout leader might be able to give you the names of some. Most parents are more than willing to talk about their child's school. Clearly, one family's response to a school does not give a complete picture and will need to be supplemented with other information, but it's a way to begin.

Your school counselor might also be helpful if a fair number of students from your child's current elementary or middle school go on to private high schools. Although they will and should be reluctant to discuss the specific academic records of other students, they can give you some sense of how students have fared in transferring to private schools.

In the next chapter we'll outline the wealth of available resources that will tell you about private schools all over the country. *Peterson's Guide to Private Secondary Schools* and Peterson's Web site include comprehensive data on more than 1,500 private schools. Almost every school publishes guides and view books that will familiarize you with its curriculum and philosophy. Most day schools schedule open houses in the fall that are free and open to the public. These are almost always advertised in the local paper and can also be learned about by calling the admissions office of any school.

Open Houses

Attending several open houses in your area, even if they aren't ones to which you anticipate applying, is a great way to learn about private schools. Most day school open houses are held on a Saturday or Sunday afternoon in the fall, last about 1½ hours, don't require preregistration, and include presentations by administrators, faculty members, and students. You'll see ads for the open houses in the local papers for several weeks before they occur, and you should feel free to call the admissions office of any school and ask for details of their event. Many include current parents and students as volunteers at these events, so prospective parents have a great opportunity to ask informal questions.

Attending several open houses given by private schools in your area, even if they aren't ones to which you will be applying, is a great way to learn about private schools.

Although these open houses are fairly relaxed, most kids wear school clothes as opposed to shorts and T-shirts. The programs often include some sort of musical performance and offer a host of written information about the school. Prospective parents and children are welcomed, although you might choose to go without your child if you're in the early, fact-finding stages of learning about private schools rather than focusing on this particular school. Some kids resent being dragged to visit a school they aren't ever going to attend, so if you sense that your child is going to have a limited appetite for this kind of event, save him for the ones that count. The last thing you want is a child who is already sick of the process before the serious looking begins. Other children find these visits stimulating and motivating. Carefully orchestrated, an open house can serve as a catalyst in getting a child to focus more on his school work to increase his chances of acceptance at the school. Most open houses present the school in an appealing way, leaving visitors eager to return and learn more.

In addition to open houses, some schools arrange a series of informational gatherings in the homes of current parents. These are usually small, informal, and a great opportunity to ask questions about carpooling, athletics, or homework. The admissions office tries to have prospective families come to a gathering close to their neighborhood so they can connect with nearby families from the school.

Families who are relocating for professional reasons find their companies to be helpful and knowledgeable about school choices in the area. Realtors are often another valuable source of information about private school options. Obviously, they may have their own personal biases and experiences but they can give you some helpful basic information. There is also a strong network of private school administrators across the country that is more than willing to recommend a list of schools for you to explore. If you're being relocated, your own principal might be helpful.

Independent School Counselors

Some people, especially those who are looking at boarding schools or are moving to an area with which they have had limited exposure, decide to hire the services of an independent school counselor. These counselors spend a great deal of time visiting and revisiting private schools, so they are familiar with the philosophy and special strengths of each school. After spending time interviewing you and your child and reviewing her records, the counselor will be able to steer you toward a list of schools that might fit well.

Families who have a particularly difficult time communicating or who feel they could use a neutral negotiator have found these counselors especially helpful. If a child or one parent is reluctant to even consider a search or has an entirely different idea of what would be a good fit, a third party might be able to intervene. There are certainly situations where either the parents or the child needs someone to lead a search and could benefit from the counselor's efforts to present the child to the schools with his best foot forward.

INCREASING YOUR CHILD'S SOCIAL SKILLS

Applying to a private school will involve some sort of interview for your child, whether it be a formal one with a member of the admissions staff or more informal, such as visiting with a tour guide, the admissions director, or the teachers of the classes he visits. Either way, the process will be less stressful and more productive if your child is comfortable interacting with adults and has acquired some basic social skills.

I would argue that it's never too early to begin teaching your child how to introduce himself, shake hands, and look someone in the eye. Even young children can learn not to interrupt, how to listen to others, and how to carry on a conversation. Shy children can be encouraged to interact with their grandparents and close family friends. Be sure that they get some airtime at the dinner table, even if they're surrounded by chattier siblings. Outside activities, such as soccer or a dance troop, will give your child a chance to get to know other adults. If your child seems particularly shy or uncomfortable around adults, you might talk with one of his favorite teachers about various strategies to overcome this.

> Erma Bombeck said she always learned the most from her kids when they were in the back seat of the car. She thought it had to do with the lack of eye contact—they felt more comfortable and spoke up.

As your child becomes more adept at talking with you and other adults he knows well, he will learn to become more comfortable meeting new people. As with many skills, we serve as models for our children. They watch us as we deal with people. They see us make an effort to put other people at ease, to reach out and include people in a conversation. Whether or not these skills come readily to your child, you may help to reinforce his efforts, to notice and compliment him on his attempts to overcome his shyness or to reach out to someone. For many children, acquiring these skills takes practice and encouragement.

As with encouraging your child to read more or finding some activities he enjoys, increasing his comfort talking with adults is something he will benefit from, whether he applies to a private school or not.

Summer Programs

Many private day schools have extensive summer programs that include both academic and recreational offerings. Attending one of these might appeal to your child and give both of you an opportunity to learn more about the campus and to feel more comfortable there. Although almost all of these summer programs include students from various schools, there will certainly be some students and teachers who are part of the school during the academic year. Getting to know them might be a great way to hear about the school in a more informal way.

Peterson's Guide to Private Secondary Schools, which we'll talk about in detail in Chapter 4, includes a comprehensive list of private schools that have summer sessions that are open to students from other schools. Having your child attend a summer session at a boarding school might be a wonderful way to look at a specific school and to get a better sense of the boarding school experience in general. Needless to say, going to a four-week summer session is a different experience than attending boarding school for four years, but it may be a helpful first step.

As you begin to learn more about private schools, you may start worrying about whether your child can get into these schools. It will be helpful to channel this natural anxiety in ways that might improve your child's chances.

Having your child attend a summer session at a boarding school might be a wonderful way to look at a specific school and to get a better sense of the boarding school experience in general.

Although some parents cringe to think of these activities, because they seem to smack of encouraging their middle school children to build their resumes, the truth is that the competition is tough and appears to be getting worse. Although all parents hope their children are working hard in school and doing their best, the desire to go to another school can be a powerful motivator. Children need to know that private schools are looking for students who work hard and do well. It's that simple. With a much larger applicant pool, fewer and fewer schools need to take chances on kids who could probably do the work but haven't chosen to work in their current school. Many admissions officers are wary of kids with fabulous standardized test scores, which suggest great potential, and low grades, which reflect poor performance.

The application to almost every private school will include a request for at least two teacher recommendations. It may be helpful to keep this in mind, especially if your child is fairly quiet and in a large class. As parents, we all hope that our child's teachers know her well and appreciate her gifts. The reality is that each child makes stronger connections with some of her teachers than with others.

Many schools will ask for recommendations from the English and math teachers, while others will give you the opportunity to choose additional teachers to write. Some schools solicit input from the middle school principal or home room teacher. In Chapter 5, we'll spend more time developing a strategy for putting these recommendations together, but it is important to realize that your child's teachers, especially those in her final year of the old school, play an important role in her application to a new school.

YOUR CHILD'S WRITING AND READING

Applications to almost every private school include some sort of writing sample. Some schools ask for three or four pieces, at least one of which is written at the school with no first drafts or help from a parent or teacher. It might be advisable to spend some time looking at your child's writing beforehand. Can he write a well-organized paragraph with reasonably accurate spelling and punctuation? Can he present an idea and then support it with some details? Can he write an introduction and a concluding paragraph?

Not all children or adults are gifted writers, and certainly some bright children have real difficulties with spelling or grammar. That said, there is no question that your child's writing will certainly be considered in his private school application.

Talk with your child's English teacher. Ask her for specific suggestions as to how he can improve. Ask how your child's writing compares to that of his classmates.

Encourage your child to write thank you notes, postcards, and letters to grandparents and friends. Keeping a trip diary or a journal could provide more experience. Find ways to encourage his efforts at creative writing, posting his stories and poems on the refrigerator. Many elementary and middle schools publish magazines or newspapers. Participating in those might interest your child and encourage his writing. Enthusiastic writers seem to enjoy sending stories or poems for publication in magazines that are specifically designed for young people. Your school or local librarian can fill you in on the specifics. Crossword puzzles and word games like *Scrabble*™ can improve vocabularies, and some kids love using magnetic letters to create poems on the refrigerator.

Encouraging Reading

Encourage your child to read. Comic books and magazines are better than nothing. Some children enjoy having their own subscription to a magazine designed for kids. Research seems to suggest that children who see their parents read a fair amount are more likely to turn into readers themselves. Unfortunately, many children today spend far too much time watching television and playing video games; they don't regain their early enthusiasm for reading until they graduate from high school. Some of our best high school students are too overprogrammed to make much time to read for pleasure. Children should at least be encouraged to spend part of their vacations curled up with a good book. I was interested to see that, in an effort to encourage reading, Princeton University was offering two season passes to athletic events to any child in grades 1 through 8 who read ten books over the summer. Parents might dream up similar schemes to encourage their own children.

Private schools constantly repeat that they are trying to teach lifelong habits, one of which is reading.

Your local librarian or a teacher with a real interest in your child can be helpful in suggesting titles or getting your child hooked on a particular series or author. Although you might not share your son's obsession with science fiction or murder mysteries, be happy that he's reading. Talking with him about what he's reading, mentioning to others that he's a great reader, and showing him brief articles in magazines and newspapers can help send the message that you think reading is important. Again, this is a lifetime habit, not a gimmick designed to get him into a bunch of private schools. Private schools constantly assert that they are trying to teach lifelong habits, and one of those is reading.

The most competitive private schools will be looking at an applicant pool that includes children who have taken the most challenging courses that were available in their schools and who have done well in those classes. There are serious drawbacks in trying to force your child into classes and sections where she will be over her head, but when given an opportunity to join an accelerated section or to participate in a special program for talented students, encourage your child.

OUTSIDE ACTIVITIES

Many applicants also will have pursued activities outside of school. Some parents get carried away with exposing their children to every activity known to man. The cynics refer to these parents as resume-padders. Whatever the title or motivation, you know the drill. Their daughter has piano Monday; ballet Tuesday; soccer Wednesday, Saturday, and

Sunday; Brownies Thursday; and so on. This usually results in an exhausted child who doesn't enjoy or do particularly well in any of these activities.

In a best-case scenario, you will help your child find between one and three activities that he really enjoys and can master. With a bit of luck, some aptitude, and a good coach, he can learn some skills, realize that practice and hard work usually lead to improvement, enjoy working with others, and feel good about the experience.

All of us like to do things we're good at; for some children, it takes a bit of shopping around before they find those things. While the traditional activities like soccer, dance, baseball, and scouts appeal to many, others find more pleasure and a sense of accomplishment in mastering Tae-Kwon-Do, figure skating, or chess. Children who are not successful at the more traditional activities sometimes need permission to stop participating and feeling like a failure. After a bad experience, it is particularly important to find another, perhaps less traditional, activity where your child can experience some success and feel better about himself.

Elementary school teachers have known a lot of different children and might be good at recommending activities that might appeal to your child. Certainly some children need to sample several before they find the right one, but signing up for a new activity every fall is a bad idea. Few children can learn about tenacity, the importance of practice and drill, and the joy of mastery if they're constantly changing instruments or sports. Too many learn early on to blame their lack of success or lack of a starring role on a bad coach, or one who "didn't like them." Even a young child can learn to accept and live with the fact that she's not the best player on the team and that she won't always play on a winning team.

Your child will benefit enormously from participating in and mastering an activity he enjoys. Adolescents spend so much of their time worrying about what their classmates think of them that it can be comforting to have an area outside of school in which to build self-esteem. Most children also enjoy having a different set of friends who don't know anything about their daily academic trials and tribulations. Getting to know a coach or music teacher outside of school can also give your child another important adult role model. Often these adults develop close, longterm relationships with the children they coach. If your child has been fortunate enough to enjoy one of these relationships, be sure to get some input from that adult as you begin your search for a good fit for you child. Even if he isn't in a position to suggest specific schools, he can probably be helpful in developing a more complete picture of your child.

> Admissions committees are just as unimpressed with resumes that are overpacked with outside activities as they are with those that have no activites on them.

Although I share the concern of many educators that children are growing up too fast and no longer spend enough time relaxing and being children, I also know that many middle school kids love being given responsibilities. Many of them enjoy babysitting, working as assistant counselors in summer camps, and volunteering at hospitals and nursing homes. Many children organize and participate in walks, bike rides, and bake sales to raise money for the homeless or victims of disasters. They like being taken seriously, being given responsibility, and being able to do something for others.

Children don't do these things to look good on their private school applications. They do them because they are genuinely interested in the project arc or interested in being with the kids who are genuinely interested in the project. Yes, these are activities that private school admissions folks will notice, but more important, they are activities that could help teach your child empathy, a sense of commitment to his community, and how to work with others. These are important lessons. Again, school counselors, friends, scout leaders, and others can give you a list of specific suggestions. Kids enjoy these experiences most when the organization is used to working with children and knows how to assign them in ways that are both productive for the organization and satisfying to the volunteers. Volunteer opportunities also provide children with another chance to interact with adults. Some kids volunteer on weekends while others have spent much of their summers this way. The possibilities are almost endless.

Other children spend at least part of their weekends or summers taking courses that are of particular interest to them or are something their schools do not offer. These run the gamut from an hour of French on Saturday mornings to a three-week computer camp at a college campus. The opportunities are extensive, but they also can be expensive. Again, your child's school, soccer coach, or music teacher would probably have information about other programs.

Some parents fall into the trap of thinking that their child must participate in an extensive, expensive summer program to impress the private school admissions officers. There are lots of local and volunteer experiences that can be equally important for your child. Again, the point is not to collect a list of impressive summer courses or activities but to find things for your child to do that will be stimulating, pleasurable, and in the best of all worlds, teach him some important lessons. Walking the dogs at the SPCA, taking your own pet to visit a nursing home, assisting for free or for minimum pay at a day-care center, or working at the Special Olympics can be wonderful opportunities for children to learn how to give of themselves.

It's interesting to see how all different kinds of children can benefit from these experiences. The popular, highly successful, and sometimes self-focused adolescent can become a little less self-centered. A shy, less socially adept kid can find another world in which he becomes more confident. Another child, who may be struggling with academics, may discover an environment where she can be more successful.

Whatever you and your child choose to explore on the weekends, after school, or in the summer, it's critical to remember that all of these projects should be secondary to your child's school work. Particularly in the most competitive schools, admissions officers are looking first at each child's academic performance and teacher comments. No child should be so overcommitted to outside activities that his school work suffers. Some parents find it hard to determine how much is too much, especially if their child seems eager to do more. Some kids want to do everything their friends do, and most are slow to recognize or admit that they're tired. If your child seems cranky, less enthusiastic, or is not doing as well at school, you might talk to her teacher about your concerns. The "It's Tuesday, it must be ballet," child can often keep up with it all for a little while but eventually becomes more stressed, starts falling asleep right after dinner, or can't sleep and loses her ability to focus on her school work. With a little moderation, much of this can be avoided.

> Resist the temptation to sign your child up for every course and activity around. This is a case where less is more. Find a few activities that your child enjoys and stick with them.

It is amazing and dismaying how many parents get caught up in the syndrome of "my child's life is busier than mine." Mom spends all her free time driving her daughter to nightly soccer practices. Mom and Dad spend almost all of every weekend attending their daughter's soccer games all over the state. She's in two leagues and on a traveling team, so she plays in at least three tournaments. The season runs six months. She is just ten years old.

The saddest part of this story can be the deep-down, real motivation. All too often someone has convinced Mom and Dad that this level of play will get their daughter into the top colleges. The same fantasy, granted at a slightly less frenetic pace, gets played out in families who are worried about getting their children into private schools.

There is no question that private schools, and particularly the most competitive ones, are looking for children who are strong students and have other skills, aptitudes, or interests. Being a soccer star is certainly a plus, but it is not a necessity.

Unless your child is especially gifted or incredibly passionate about a particular sport or activity, you'd be wise to carefully consider the amount of time she commits to any activity. It strikes me as a bit bizarre when an entire family's schedule for months on end rotates around a ten-year old's soccer schedule. No wonder these children are devastated when they lose or are too exhausted to enjoy or be interested in anything else.

STANDARDIZED TESTING

In addition to your child's grades and activities, admissions officers will be interested in your child's standardized test scores. Although not all private schools require applicants to take the Secondary School Admission Test (SSAT), or the Independent School Entrance Examination (ISEE), the number that do is growing. Even thinking about taking a standardized test can raise the anxiety level in many children and adults. While admissions decisions do not turn on these results alone, and most admission directors would be quick to assure a candidate that many other factors are carefully studied, strong test scores will enhance any child's candidacy to a competitive private school.

> Like it or not, your child's standardized test scores will be taken into consideration by private schools. There are some strategies that may help improve test scores, but it's most important to find schools where students with similar scores flourish.

Some schools pay a great deal of attention to SSAT scores, while others consider them as only one of a handful of important features of a child's application. Both the SSAT and the ISEE cover four major areas: Verbal Analysis, Mathematics, Reading Comprehension, and Essay Writing. The questions are multiple-choice, with five choices for each question on the SSAT and four choices on the ISEE. Being able to compare a student's scores on a standardized test with children the same age all over the country allows a school to compare candidates who have never met or taken the same course.

SSAT

The SSAT takes more than two hours and is given on selected Saturdays in November, December, January, February, March, April, and June at more than 600 test locations around the United States. It is given in seventy-six other countries in November, January, and April. Students also have the opportunity to take the test year-round at some sites and in twelve urban areas that have Independent Test Centers. You can get a free copy of the *SSAT Student Guide* at SSATB, 12 Stockton Street, Princeton, NJ 08540 (800-442-SSAT) that includes a test registration form and all the details about where and when the tests are given. You can also request a copy of *Preparing for the SSAT*, which includes tests for student practice.

ISEE

Some schools use the ISEE, the Educational Records Bureau's Independent School Entrance Exam. It takes about three hours and is given to kids applying to grades 9 through 12 as a way to measure their aptitude and achievement in math and verbal areas. The ISEE also has multiple choice questions and a 30-minute essay. Although the essay is not scored with the rest of the test, it does give each school a chance to see how each applicant writes. The ISEE can also be taken at different schools across the United States. Write to the Educational Records Bureau, 345 E. 47th Street, New York, NY 10017 (800-989-3721) to receive a free guide with all the test details, including dates and locations.

Preparing For the Tests

Not unlike the SAT, which high school students take to apply for college, the SSAT is administered several times each year, so a student may take it more than once in an effort to improve his scores. One way to help boost your child's score is to encourage him to practice with sample tests. These sample tests, which are available in test preparation books like *Peterson's SSAT/ISEE Success*, can be helpful to children, most of whom don't like standardized tests and are nervous that poor results might prevent them from getting accepted to a school they want to attend. Being familiar with the test's questions and suggestions for answering them will certainly reduce some anxiety.

Crossword puzzlers can readily identify with the advantages of having worked many puzzles. You begin to look for certain patterns and become more confident about how to attack a puzzle. These books also offers important test-taking strategies, such as not spending a lot of time on hard questions, but rather skipping them and, if you have time at the end, returning to them then. Each question has the same value, and you aren't penalized for any unanswered questions. You do lose ¼ point for each incorrect answer. Given that grading system, it's smart to only answer those questions for which you have a fairly good idea of the answer. Wild guessing when you can't eliminate any of the five choices isn't a good idea.

That might sound pretty obvious to those of us who have taken lots of standardized tests and are greatly relieved to know that, barring some truly unforseen and dreadful circumstances, we will never take another one. For middle school kids who haven't had a great deal of standardized test experience and have probably not paid much attention to the few they have taken, being armed with these strategies will be reassuring.

The SSAT is divided into four sections: the student is asked to write a 25-minute essay on a given topic, analyze 30 synonyms and 30 analogies (25 minutes), complete 50 math problems (25 minutes), and read 7 passages and answer questions about them (25 minutes).

The ISEE is similar but is divided into five sections. Students write an essay (30 minutes), work with 20 synonyms, complete 20 sentences (20 minutes), and work

Some schools pay a lot of attention to SSAT and ISEE scores, while others consider them as only one of a handful of important features on a child's application.

on two different sections that test their quantitative ability and achievement (35 minutes; 40 minutes).

Even a cursory flip through the practice questions will reveal the advantages a strong reader will have. Being familiar with synonyms and understanding analogies will make the tests seem more manageable. There is no question that children who read a lot tend to have larger, more sophisticated vocabularies than their read-only-what-is-required classmates.

Although they make some exceptions every year, many schools expect the scores of their accepted candidates to fall within a certain range. They have found that children with these scores are most likely to be successful meeting the academic demands of their school. Many schools also use these standardized test scores to determine placement in different courses and sections. Knowing your child's scores and the range of the scores each school is usually considering will help you put together a list of schools where your child would have a fairly good chance of being accepted and able to manage and benefit from the program.

That said, some schools will often take a chance on a child with lower test scores but terrific grades and outstanding teacher recommendations. Needless to say, schools are less enthusiastic about students with high scores, a poor school performance, and less-than-enthusiastic teacher comments.

Motivating a smart child who is not working up to her potential can be complicated, and while switching schools may help, it is not always the panacea that parents hope for. In today's competitive market, these kids do not fare as well as they did a decade ago, when private schools were worried about filling all their seats.

The least you can do is let your child know that the combination of high test scores and poor grades will raise some questions in private school and college admissions offices. Often, hard data is more persuasive to adolescents than parental advice. An independent counselor, an admired teacher, or the middle school counselor or principal may be able to impress your child with the acceptance rates of other students with an academic profile similar to hers.

Although some students with low scores do not improve their scores by retaking the test, others do. Being more familiar with the testing process (the location, etc.) and the test itself and taking the time to do a series of practice tests can make a tremendous difference to some students.

Your child's attitude towards this "do it again and you'll do better" scheme will make a real difference. A child who is really committed to improving her score has a much greater chance of getting better results than a child who is dragged into the process. My guess is that all children will benefit from doing some of the practice exercises. Some children are in public schools that require students to take standardized tests every year, and these kids may not experience quite the same anxiety, but most kids will be anxious about this part of the process.

In addition to answering some of the available practice questions, there are other things your child should do:

1. Get a good night's sleep before the test. (Save the slumber party for the night after the test.)

2. Locate your registration ticket, No. 2 pencils, and other required materials the night before.

3. Eat a nutritious breakfast (not potato chips and a candy bar).

4. Get good directions to the test site. (You don't need the extra stress of getting lost.)

5. Get there early.

6. Dress comfortably and be prepared for a room that will be either too hot or too cold.

Some bright kids don't do well on standardized tests and never will. If your child's scores are not as high as you anticipated or hoped, it might be helpful to talk about them with your middle school principal or classroom teacher. He can help you put them in some kind of context and relate them to your child's day-to-day academic performance.

Knowing your child's SSAT or ISEE scores will give you a better sense of which schools might be a good fit for him.

Contrary to the stereotypes, the good news is there are many private schools that are not only geared for kids with all As and the highest standardized test scores. Knowing your child's SSAT or ISEE scores will help you have a better sense of which schools might be a good fit for him. Remember, you are looking for schools where he has a fairly good chance of being accepted and then being successful. Some schools include in their admission materials the mean scores of the students they accept. Although there are exceptions every year, these should give you some sense of the guidelines they will be using.

Parents should also keep in mind that there are a number of programs out there that are designed to accommodate underachievers. Still other programs are created specifically for students who need remedial work in math or who are learning disabled. You can find information on this kind of school listed in *Peterson's Guide to Private Secondary Schools.* Although their average test scores seem to be a little harder to get hold of than from their competitive counterparts, you can certainly talk with their admissions directors about the academic profile of children they can best serve.

Assuming that you've had some time to think about your child and his academic profile as well as the reasons why you're interested in a private school, it's time to start developing a short list of possible schools.

Lifelong Skills to Help Your Child Be a Strong Candidate

- Encourage her to read (comics and magazines are better than nothing).

- Discourage TV.

- Encourage her to write (a diary, journal, letters).

- Pursue a limited number of activities that she enjoys.

- Encourage volunteering (or paid jobs) to develop responsibility and self-confidence.

- Find ways to encourage her to be at ease with adults.

Learning About Private Schools

Gathering good information about private schools can be a daunting task. Fortunately, there is a wealth of printed information that will help you in your search for a private school. *Peterson's Guide to Private Secondry Schools* includes a comprehensive listing of over 1,800 private schools in the United States and Canada. A brief review of each school includes up-to-date information about its program, facilities, range of grade levels, faculty, college placement, and special opportunities.

This book also provides specialized directories that group schools according to type, entrance requirements, curricula, and financial aid data. Although the size of the book, more than 1,400 pages, may at first seem overwhelming, it is comprehensive and helpful. Some families have been particularly grateful for its inclusion of schools with programs for students with special needs and of schools that accommodate underachievers.

Web Sites

If you enjoy surfing the web, you could make good use of www.petersons.com, where you will find four-color view books and descriptions of hundreds of private high schools. You can also request information about specific schools that interest you. Many schools now have their own web sites, which include tours of the campus, course descriptions, weekly events, and up-to-the-minute athletic results.

Some include extensive information about their admissions policies and practices and allow you the option of requesting a catalogue and application on line. Others include interviews with the Head of School and a section of frequently asked questions about the school. The most elaborate even provide interactive tours of the campus, and all of them provide a more complete picture of the school than what you can learn from just browsing through the printed materials.

Needless to say, a small or less affluent school may not have a Web site, or if it does, it may not be very elaborate. Although the information and pictures on the Web sites may be helpful, don't make assumptions about a school that doesn't have a Web site. Some small, wonderful schools don't have the financial or technological resources to develop a Web site.

Videos

Following the example of many colleges, some schools, primarily boarding schools, have put together excellent videos that will give you a good sense of the campus, the facilities, and at least a snapshot of some teachers and students. Clearly no video, Web site, or catalog can present the same comprehensive, unrehearsed look at a school as you get when you visit. But when you are considering schools at a considerable distance, these tools can be helpful. Obviously they are promotional pieces designed to show each school at its best. Expect to see only carefully edited pictures of a manicured campus and happy, attractive students interacting with teachers who look genuinely interested and concerned about these children. While the pictures may present a realistic view of the school, you'll probably want to see it for yourself.

Families considering boarding schools can get a free
copy of the Boarding Schools Directory from the National
Association of Independent Schools, 1620 L Street, NW,
Washington, D.C., 20036-5605 (202-973-9700).

Written Materials

As you hear or read about a school that interests you, look
it up in print or on the Web and contact the admissions
office to request a catalog and application. Most private
schools spend a good deal of money and time producing
attractive catalogs that showcase their students, campus,
and programs. Although they vary with the size and resources
of the school, these view books tell you a fair amount about
the school's philosophy and what it considers its strengths
and selling points. Most include descriptions of the required
and elective courses, athletic and extracurricular offerings,
and their college placement.

Reading carefully through each catalog will tell you a
great deal about the specific school and, perhaps equally
important, will provide you with some criteria for compar-
ing and contrasting schools. You'll see lots of similarities in
programs, values, activities, and even photographs. But as
you read more closely, you'll also notice the ways in which
the schools are different.

Course Descriptions

Most middle school students are immediately drawn to the
lists of unusual (and usually elective) courses such as
philosophy, psychology, and ecology, but you can learn a
lot about a school from the list of required courses as well.

Almost every school requires four years of English, although many include some interesting choices for juniors and seniors within the English curriculum. Some offer English trimester courses that allow older students to select three separate courses each year. This seems to be an effective way to be sure that every student has studied a range of literature while also allowing students to pursue the areas that most appeal to them. Although many schools have spent hours debating the pros and cons of semesters versus trimesters, both calendars work well and parents needn't worry about which one a school follows.

Driven in part by admissions offices of the most competitive colleges, more and more of the strongest high school students are taking four years of science and math. Many private high schools require all their students to take two years of science, one of which must be a lab course. Strong science students will be looking for a program that includes different levels of biology, chemistry, and physics, with the possibility of honors work. Schools that emphasize science usually provide opportunities for their students to compete in science olympiads and competitions.

A list of the math courses each school offers will shed light on the type of students they enroll. Many schools offer several sections of Algebra I to their ninth graders while other schools expect their students to have already completed Algebra I. The academic powerhouses usually include AB and BC calculus and perhaps an advanced topics course for their strongest mathematicians. If your child is gifted in math, check to see if a school offers these advanced courses every year or just when there is sufficient demand. You will probably notice mention of student participation in various math leagues and contests in the literature of schools with a strong emphasis on math.

> Be sure to request a copy of a school's curriculum—you can learn a lot about a school from the courses they require students to take.

If you are looking for a private school for your daughter, ask about the number of girls in the upper-level math classes. Many all-girls schools will make special note of the advantages of teaching math in all-girl classes where students might have a better chance of developing their self-confidence and fulfilling their mathematical aptitude.

Most private high schools require two or three years of a foreign language and are experiencing increasing numbers of students choosing Spanish and Latin, while French, German, Russian, Japanese, and Chinese are dropping, perhaps because some students find these to be more difficult languages to master. Recognizing the value of living where you must use the language you have studied, many of the larger schools offer a variety of opportunities to visit or study in Europe, Central America, or the Far East. Ranging from week-long visits during spring break to semester or even year-long programs where students live with families and attend the local school, these can be wonderful experiences that give real meaning to a child's study of a foreign language. As you begin to narrow your focus to just a few schools, find out how many students usually participate in these overseas opportunities. These programs can be expensive, so explore financial aid possibilities for them.

> Private school graduates often say that their schools' focus on writing, both creative and expository, gave them a real edge when they entered college.

Advanced Placement Courses

If your child is a strong student, you'll probably be looking at schools that include a large number of Advanced Placement courses (designated AP in curriculum guides). Enrollment in these courses is usually limited and by invitation. At the end of each course, students take a national exam and have the opportunity to earn college credits for their work. AP exams are graded from 1 to 5 (5 being the highest). Almost all colleges give credit for grades of 4 and 5 in these exams and some give credit for a score of 3. Some secondary schools include information about the average grades their students (usually juniors and seniors) earn on these exams. These exams are difficult, so if a good number of their students distinguish themselves, schools are eager to show that a high percentage of their students are well-enough prepared to receive college credit for the work they did in high school. Some students have entered college with more than one year of credits.

For a host of valid reasons, a few strong private schools have chosen not to include AP courses in their curriculum. Don't automatically misread their omission as a sign of a less-competitive school. These schools have usually chosen to offer a series of honors courses in lieu of the APs, which will be indicated in their curriculum guide. As you narrow your focus, you may want to ask about the AP course opportunities. Although some schools list some 15 AP courses, a closer study will show that not all of these courses are offered every year and that many have few students. If a school chooses to offer AP courses, and has twelve or more AP courses each year with full enrollments, it would be fair to assume it has a rigorous academic program.

Faculty

School guidebooks often include a list of all the teachers and the year in which they joined the school. At strong, stable schools you can expect to see a good mix of 20-year-plus veterans and new teachers. Read through the list of faculty members and note where they were trained and how many of them have advanced degrees. Schools with national reputations usually attract faculty mambers from universities across the country. Smaller schools and those with limited financial resources are often unable to attract as diverse a group of teachers. Although you certainly want to know that your child's teachers are well educated and interested in pursuing their own education at the graduate level, a teacher's degree doesn't really tell you anything about one's effectiveness as a teacher.

A SCHOOL'S EMPHASIS

Guide books often include lists of faculty members, extracurricular offerings, and athletic programs. It's interesting to see which programs are highlighted and where the school's emphasis lies. You can learn a lot about a school by looking at the awards they give and the materials they choose to send you. If they're not included in the initial packet, ask to see a copy of the school newspaper and literary magazine. What do the students write about? How well do they write? What do they see as major issues? Who gets recognized and applauded in the student publications? This can tell you a bit more about the school's culture.

Needless to say, every school wants to publish its college information in ways that will interest and impress prospective families. You need to read the data carefully to be sure you know what it does and doesn't mean.

Arts

If your child is particularly interested in the arts, note how many drama productions the school puts on each year. How many art shows, musical revues, and student-written or -directed pieces? Are students encouraged to submit their work to shows and galleries outside of school? How high a profile do the singing groups have? Do they have travel opportunities comparable to those of the athletic teams? Do they perform in local nursing homes or in juried competitions? Does the school have a band or orchestra that receives student and faculty member support and interest?

Although most private schools require all their students to have some exposure to the arts, a quick review of the academic and nonacademic programs of each school should give you some sense of their emphasis on the arts. Large schools have remarkable arts facilities that allow them to offer a wide range of courses that might include photography, ceramics, painting, filmmaking, and woodworking. Others have the resources to offer a wide range of dance, movement, acting, and directing opportunities. Given your child's experience, interest, and talent, it is important to find out more about the number of kids who take these courses. Six schools could include photography in their list of courses,but for each it could represent a different range of opportunities. In one school it may only mean an introductory course, pursued mostly by ninth graders; at another school it may refer to an elective that is open only to seniors; at yet another school it refers to a popular set of courses designed to allow many students to progress to an advanced level.

Athletics

Your athletic child will want to check out the number of sports a school offers, whether freshmen can play on varsity teams, and whether the school is large enough to field a junior varsity or third team. Kids who initially seem reluctant to leave their neighborhood schools may become intrigued when they read about schools that offer fencing, ice hockey, and golf teams. See which schools publish the percentage of their kids who participate in the athletic programs. Most schools offer both interscholastic (competing with other schools) and intramural (competition against classmates) opportunities.

Both boarding and day schools—but primarily those with some boarding students—include a number of post graduates (PGs) who have completed four years of high school and are taking an additional year, often to position themselves to be stronger candidates for college. The participation of PGs on high school teams can both improve the performance of these teams and make it harder for underclassmen to make a varsity team. For some athletes, it can be frustrating to find that three or four of the starting positions each season are taken by PG students. If your child is athletic and hoping to play at the varsity level, learn more about each school's policies and experience with PGs.

Your nonathletic, perhaps even PE-phobic child, may be relieved to read about a variety of options by which he can satisfy his PE and athletic requirements. He may also be drawn to smaller schools where a higher percent of kids are needed to play on the school teams or schools that offer a wide range of intramural sports. Students who are particularly interested in dance, gymnastics, or figure skating should explore whether these activities can fulfill their athletic requirements. Many schools have specific guidelines for students who are pursuing an individual sport.

Exchange Programs

Many private school guidebooks also describe opportunities for students to study at other schools, often in other countries. A number of large boarding schools allow their students to spend part of a year in programs like the Swiss Semester, City Term (The Master's School), or the Mountain

School (Milton Academy). Knowing how many kids participate in these programs each year should give you more insight into whether this is part of the typical experience or something that only involves one or two children a year. Also find out about the costs of these programs because, like the foreign language trips, sometimes there is only a limited amount of financial aid available, and they can be quite expensive.

Some private schools have established consortiums that allow students to spend part of a year attending a school in another part of the country, living with another family at no cost beyond transportation. The Sacred Heart schools have such a relationship (Network of Sacred Heart Schools), as do a group of day schools who have organized the Domestic Exchange. This exchange encourages kids to spend part of their year in a similar private school but in a different part of the country. The Domestic Exchange includes, among others, Lakeside School in Seattle, Albuquerque Academy, Princeton Day School, and St. John's in Texas. Any one of these schools could give you more information.

Community Service

Given their freedom to focus on values and character development, most private schools have designed specific programs to foster leadership, teach decision making, and provide drug and alcohol education. Although many schools will list these courses in their guides, you'll get a greater sense of their importance in the community as you read the school newspaper, the newsletter, and any parent publications. Many private schools pride themselves on their community service programs, but again, to have a better sense of these programs, you'll want to find out how many students participate, how important these programs seem to be to both the kids and their teachers, and whether there is any effort to incorporate this service into the academic curriculum. Recent research has suggested that service learning (connecting appropriate community service to the study of a specific novel or period of history) can be the most effective way to teach the text and to give real meaning to serving others. In recent years many schools have added a community service component to their requirements for graduation. It is not unusual for students to do 40 to 50 hours of service during their high school careers.

Religious Schools

Many families are interested in the moral and spiritual education their children will be receiving. You'll need to look at each school individually. For example, the Friends schools share similar Quaker philosophies and a commitment to a multi-cultural community where everyone feels included. Each school has its individual character and ethos. Contact the Friends Council on Education for more information.

Similarly, there is a wide range of schools with affiliations with the Episcopal Church. Some of these schools require chapel and religious courses are while others are nondenominational and have no academic religious requirements. (You can get more information from the National Association of Episcopal Schools.) You will learn a great deal about the religious life of a school from its philosophy and various publications, but visiting the campus is an important way to understand the role of religion at the school. Feel free to ask the admissions officer as well as students or faculty members about their experiences with the religious aspect of the school. It's critical that you have a good understanding of what to expect at each of the schools you're considering. This issue could have a profound impact on whether you and your child will be comfortable.

Military Schools

Some families are also interested in learning more about military schools and although their numbers have diminished in the past decade, they have been a successful match for some children. These schools pride themselves on providing structure and discipline for adolescents who need help organizing their learning. Contrary to the stereotype that was more appropriate ten years ago, military schools are not interested in shaping up kids with serious discipline issues. Many are now coed and include day students as well as boarders. Students wear uniforms, the atmosphere is less casual than many other independent schools, and the curriculum usually includes some study of military history.

Many military schools also have a religious affiliation. Although more of their graduates apply to the service academies (West Point, the Naval Academy, the Air Force Academy) than seniors in other independent schools, their graduates go to a wide range of schools and universities.

Each of these schools has its own ethos and personality, so if you are interested in exploring this type of school, be sure to visit several. Although there certainly may be some unusual situations that make it necessary to send your child to a military school against his wishes, it will probably be a better match if your child has some interest in exploring this option. Contact the Association of Military Colleges and Schools of the United States (301-765-0695) for more information.

Contrary to the stereotype that was more appropriate ten years ago, military schools are not interested in shaping up kids with serious discipline issues.

Special Schools

You may already know, or discover during your search for a private school, that your child has special needs or an unusual learning style. Some families are fortunate to either recognize themselves or have it pointed out to them by perceptive teachers that their young child has some learning issues. Unhappily, sometimes these discoveries are not made until a child enters adolescence.

Some teachers are quite skilled at recognizing, assessing, and helping to address different learning styles. Others are not. As you might expect, certain public and private schools are better than others at accommodating children with learning issues. If your child has an unusual learning style, is dyslexic, or is suffering from ADD, it's important that he be in a school that is equipped to help him.

If your child is struggling in school and there seems to be a wide gap between his perceived aptitude and his performance, you should certainly raise those issues with his teacher or adviser. A formal evaluation can be expensive, but it's important to have a professional assessment if dyslexia, ADD, or other learning disabilities are suspected. These assessments will reveal the extent of the problem and almost always include specific recommendations for the student and suggested accommodations for the faculty members. Contact the Orton Dyslexia Society at 212-691-1930 for more information.

The good news is that there are lots of private schools that are skilled at and eager to work with kids with dyslexia, ADD, and a host of other academic and emotional issues.

Some parents are slow to go down this path, hoping that if the problem isn't diagnosed and labeled, it will go away. Others are convinced that any learning issue can be cured by hard work. This is not always true. Unfortunately, other parents involved in a private school search are convinced that their child would be better served if they don't reveal any diagnosis or report to the schools to which they're applying, which is a bad idea because eventually the issue will resurface in the new school and valuable time will have been wasted.

The good news is that there are private schools that are skilled at and eager to work with kids with dyslexia, ADD, and other academic and emotional issues. These schools include day, boarding, coed, and single-sex institutions. They are all over the country, often require no application fee, do require an interview on campus, and will often accept and enroll students throughout the school year.

You will need to review, visit, and learn about these schools in much the same way you learn about other private schools. Most will be eager to share with you the names of families to contact whose children went to that school and thrived. Those personal recommendations are even more important when you know your child has some unusual issues that need to be addressed.

Don't Despair

At this point, you may feel like you'll have to quit your job and put your other children up for adoption in order to have the time required to learn about private schools. Not true. I'm raising these questions not to suggest that you will want or need to pursue them, but rather to point out that similar program descriptions or lists may mean different things at different schools. You and your child may want to learn more about the programs that interest you to have a better sense of what each school really offers. I'm not suggesting you write all these questions down on a huge list and march in to the admissions office demanding answers. They'd view you as a nightmare come true. But thinking about these questions may help you determine what matters to you and inspire a careful reading of each school's literature.

ACCOUNTABILITY OF PRIVATE SCHOOLS

Many public school families are surprised and dismayed to learn that private schools are not evaluated in any formal way that ranks or compares them with each other. Many choose to be accredited by one of several accrediting organizations, such as the Middle States Association of Schools and Colleges and the New England Association of Schools and Colleges. These accreditations focus on whether the school is actually doing what it claims to be doing. In other words, are its programs in concert with its mission and philosophy. The accreditation group does not judge the value or appropriateness of that mission or philosophy. It is only charged with determining whether the school is following its mission. Each accreditation involves an extensive yearlong self-study by the school, including hundreds of pages of documentation, a several-day visit by a team of private and public school teachers and administrators, a written report, and approval for accreditation. Although the process is helpful to a school in that the administrators and faculty members are forced to scrutinize their school's philosophy and programs and learn a great deal from their accreditation team about other schools and programs, the process offers little in the way of allowing parents to compare one school with another.

One could argue that, even without a ranking system or report card that grades a school or its faculty, curriculum, and discipline system, independent schools are highly accountable. They must answer daily to the parents who have chosen to pay handsomely to send them their children. Just like you, these independent school parents have opted out of the public sector because they expect and demand a better education for their children. Independent schools are constantly being scrutinized and judged by their students' families, who are customers that are both emotionally and financially invested in making sure they get what they are paying for.

Private schools also list their memberships in local associations, such as the Association of Independent Maryland Schools, or national groups, such as the National Association of Independent Schools, which includes over 1,000 schools in the United States and thirty eight other countries. To be eligible for NAIS membership, a school must be independently governed by a board of trustees, practice nondiscriminatory policies, hold not-for-profit tax status, and be accredited by an approved state or regional association. Schools find these associations to be invaluable resources for their administrators and faculty members. Many parents like knowing that their school is in contact with and is learning from the experiences of other private schools around the country. As you read about more schools, you will find that most of them with any national recognition belong to NAIS.

> **To be eligible for NAIS membership, a school must be independently governed by a board of trustees, practice nondiscriminatory policies, hold not-for-profit tax status, and be accredited by an approved state or regional association.**

There is no question that schools benefit from these regional associations, and all the well known, highly competitive private schools belong to them, but the fact that a school belongs to an association is not helpful in a parent's effort to compare and contrast the experience her child would have at School A as opposed to School B.

Rankings

Like many other educators, I am dismayed by our culture's insatiable craving for ranking lists, be that the *Best 100 Books* or the *Best Colleges* or *Hospitals*. In ranking high schools, I think it is impossible to determine what we mean by, "the best." Are we looking for the schools that are the hardest to get into? Schools that send the most graduates to the Ivy League? Schools that have the highest SAT scores? Schools that have the richest or most successful graduates? Schools that receive the most support from their graduates? Schools with the best athletic records or the most National Merit Scholars?

All of these lists might be interesting to read, but I'm not sure they would be helpful in trying to find schools where your child would fit best. Your child's fit, sense of self, and success at a school is complicated and multi-faceted. If your child is bright and an excellent student, she may do well at almost any school, but given her individual talents, personality, and interests, she may fit better in some schools than in others. You want to look for the schools that are best for your child.

You want your child to be challenged, the academics to be demanding, the faculty members experienced, and the achievements of the graduates to be impressive. But no matter how much reading and talking you do about schools,

The feel of the school, what it's like to be there day in and day out, will have a greater impact on your child's happiness and productivity than its list of SAT scores, AP courses, and college acceptances.

you need to visit them to get a real sense of the school, its values, and its ethos. The feel of the school, what it's like to be there day in and day out, will have a greater impact on your child's happiness and productivity than its list of SAT scores, AP courses, and college acceptances. Fit goes beyond factual hard data. It has to do with student-to-student and faculty-to-student interactions and relationships. It has to do with a school's culture, its expectations, and its rewards.

COLLEGE DATA

Just as you have to read each school's description of its curriculum carefully, you also need to pay close attention to what it says about college placement. Some recent articles have suggested that some of the information that private schools provide about college placement can be misleading. As with all the information a school sends to prospective families, the school wants it to be accurate and to portray the school at its best. You will not come across a school catalog that claims to send 80 percent of their graduates to the most competitive colleges and 2 percent to "terrible" colleges. On the other hand, you just need to read what it does say carefully:

"92 students graduated in 1998; 91 planned to attend college, including Brown University, the University of Pennsylvania, and Yale University."

and

"92 students graduated in 1998. Four or more are attending Brown, Colgate, Cornell, Harvard, Maryland, and Princeton."

These kinds of lists and numbers are helpful because they show you where most of a school's graduates are going rather than the fact that one student out of the last four graduating classes went to a school with which you might be familiar.

The college list for a school that emphasizes its arts program will probably include some of the colleges known for the arts. Although it's tempting to read too much into a school's college list, there are a few generalizations that hold true for most private schools. If a school consistently sends more than three or four students to MIT, you can assume it has attracted some students who are talented in math and science. If a school can consistently send three or four students to Cooper Union, Rhode Island School of Design, and the Tisch School of New York University, you can assume the school has some attractive, sophisticated arts offerings. Private schools that consistently graduate more than three or four athletes who are recruited to play at Division I colleges must have strong athletic programs. Again, if this information is important to you, you will ferret out what sports these athletes played, what specific areas these artists pursued.

It's also true that a high school counselor who sends a lot of kids to the same four or five colleges each year has established a fairly good rapport with those colleges and has a good sense of their strengths and their admissions policies. But no matter how strong the relationship between high school and college, that alone will no longer guarantee admissions. Your child will have to be accepted on his or her own performance.

SAT Data

Private schools traditionally publish information about the scores their students receive. Most college-bound juniors and seniors take the SAT, although some, primarily in the western part of the United States, take the ACT. As with the other college information, it is important to read the schools' statements carefully. SATs are scored from 200 to 800 and ACTs range from 1 to 36. Some private schools report average scores in verbal and math while others also include the percentage of the class that scored over 600 on the SAT verbal and the percentage of the class that scored over 600 on the math SAT. These are not always the same students. Almost all colleges publish comparable SAT information about their students, so this is a fairly simple way to get a sense of the kind of colleges to which a certain group of students might apply.

Some schools also publish the range of their SAT scores from the lowest to the highest any student received. In most cases a larger range will indicate that the school has a larger range of students, some of whom may be brilliant (scoring over 700), while others (scoring around 500) are closer to the average scores of college-bound seniors. Although some schools do record their mean SAT scores as well, these are not terribly helpful because they only tell you that half the class scored higher than the mean and the rest scored below it. You have no idea whether there is a huge range of scores or whether most of them are clustered right around that mean score.

Many schools also publish the number of students who are recognized for their outstanding SAT scores. This recognition includes Commended Scholars and National Merit Semi-Finalists and Finalists, who are in the top 5 percent of all the students taking the PSATs (the "practice" version of the SATs that are taken during the junior year of high school). The most competitive private schools consistently graduate classes that include an impressive number of kids who have earned this national recognition.

As you read and learned about of private schools, you will find that several specific schools pique your interest. It may be that friends have suggested the same school, that you have some personal connections to the school, or be that their written materials seem incredibly inviting. For any of these schools that seem to be rising to the top of your list, it's important that you get as much written material as you can. Again, you don't need to read every word that was ever published, but you should at least see a catalog, some description of the courses and, if possible, a copy of the application.

Although we're not ready to start filling out applications, they, like almost any other school publication, can tell you something about the school and what it values. Back when I applied to college, I recall filling out one particular application. It wasn't until I got to the eighth essay, which asked me to describe a significant experience I had had with a piece of sculpture, that I realized this excellent college was probably not a good fit for me.

Once you've collected a reasonable amount of information, you may need to force yourself to go to the next step and focus on a shorter list of schools. Some children and parents find it difficult to move to this next step. They find it tempting and less stressful to just keep collecting information rather than setting priorities and focusing on a few schools that look like the most promising fits.

It's time for us to begin to construct that shorter list.

A Short List

Now that you've accumulated a host of materials and opinions about a wide range of schools, you need to focus on how to narrow down your choices and come up with a reasonably short list of schools to visit. This is critical. No matter how good and comprehensive the literature is, you can't really understand a school's culture until you walk on its campus. That said, it's also probably true that neither you nor your child can take the time to visit dozens of schools. Your child needs to focus on his current academic work, and missing a lot of school to visit schools that he's really not interested in is a waste of time. You'll need to be selective and to keep in mind that many schools *require* students to visit as part of the admissions process.

If you're looking at local private day schools and are fortunate to have enough good choices to select from, visit three or four. Most day schools offer a number of visiting dates, but as they book them on a first-come, first-served basis, call each admissions office in late August or early September. Many boarding schools that receive large numbers of campus visitors suggest that you visit the school in the spring or summer of the year before you apply. If you can't visit until early fall, be sure to call early in the summer to schedule your appointment. Almost all schools have a standard visit, which includes a tour, an interview, perhaps time to prepare a writing sample, and time to talk with a few students or teachers. If your child is particularly interested in one or two classes or programs, be sure to mention it in your initial call so the admissions office can include them in your tour. Some schools will ask you to fill out a preliminary previsit form that includes questions about your child's specific interests.

In an ideal search—and most of them are far from systematic and on schedule—by the summer before your child's eighth grade year, you will have gathered together a fair amount of information about schools that offer the type of program you are seeking. As you put together this list, you will no doubt be wondering whether your child can get into any of these schools. Although it is a challenge to determine her chances of being accepted and being successful at each of the schools, you can get some clues from the school's literature.

YOUR CHILD'S CHANCES OF ACCEPTANCE

Many schools publish the range of test scores of their accepted students as well as the number of applications and acceptances for each grade. If these statistics are not readily available in the literature, you should feel free to raise these questions on the phone with someone from the admissions office. Giving the admissions officer a brief snapshot of your child's academic profile, including his standardized test scores and grades, might make it possible for her to at least give you some sense of whether your child belongs in the applicant pool or not and give you an idea of the kind of students with whom your child would be competing.

Given the increased number of applicants, many qualified applicants who would have been easily admitted two or three years ago are now often waitlisted. Waitlisted candidates are qualified for admission, but there simply are not enough open spots available.

In many schools, the application-to-accept ratio for the ninth grade is 4:1, while in other grades the ratio may be 15:1, with perhaps only a single opening. Be sure to ask the admissions office for the application-to-accept ratios of the previous year. Admissions officers want you to like their school, but they also want you to have a realistic sense of the admissions picture.

By now you have thought a great deal about your child and the kind of school that will serve her best, about private schools in general, and about a group of schools in particular, to create a short list of schools to which your child will apply. Although you certainly want to encourage her to stretch and apply to schools that interest her but where she might not be accepted (reaches), you also want to include schools where she has a pretty good chance of acceptance (targets) and one or two where you can be almost assured of her acceptance (safeties).

> Many schools readily acknowledge that they give priority to candidates who have relatives who attend or attended the school.

Perhaps it would be helpful to talk a little more about how to determine if a particular school is a reach, a target, or a safety for your child. The bad news is that acceptance to any private school is not based on a simple, fail-safe formula. The good news is that acceptance to any private school can be a little idiosyncratic.

You can begin by looking at the hard data: your child's grades and test scores. How do these compare to the average scores and grades of students who have been accepted at each school? Then, consider how you think your child's teachers will describe her. Try to be objective and to remember what they've said about her potential and performance before.

That hard data is usually considered first, but certainly your child may have some attributes that can make her a stronger candidate. If she's a recognized leader, a star athlete, a promising artist, or one of those unusually mature children who has already discovered the joy of service to others, she will be of greater interest to an admissions committee.

Most schools accept their students "need blind," meaning that whether or not you need financial aid won't be a factor in the school's decision to accept your child. Some of the largest private schools have sufficient financial resources to provide aid to all of their accepted students who need it. Unfortunately because of limited financial aid, some schools accept children but are not able to give them sufficient aid to attend. We'll talk about all these financial issues in much greater detail in Chapter 6.

Reaches

In making up your short list of schools, you need to classify as a "reach" any school where the hard data suggests that your child, and this is always difficult for any parent to acknowledge, probably does not have a good chance of being accepted.

Given most parents' inclination to protect their children from disappointments, it might be tempting to eliminate any reaches right from the start. One could argue that it would be better, or perhaps kinder, to avoid having your child fall in love with a school only to find out she can't go there. Each family needs to make that call on a case-by-case basis.

I would argue that there's a lot to be said for teaching our children to set lofty goals, to be willing to run the risk of disappointment. For many children, this will be the first time they haven't been able to have something they want. That's not all bad, and coping with that reality is an important part of growing up.

It would be helpful and less hurtful to candidly talk with your child about how she might not be accepted at these reach schools but that you think she should go ahead and try. Because every school is looking for a diverse group of students, each year many schools accept candidates whose acceptance would not have been easy to predict.

Targets

Determining your target schools becomes even more important if your reach schools seem out of reach. Again, begin with your child's hard data and each school's normal guidelines for acceptance. Your target schools should be ones where all indications would suggest that your child has a pretty good chance of being accepted and doing well there. If your classifications of reach, target, or safety have been fairly accurate, one could assume that your child might end up attending one of his target schools. Therefore, it's important that these be schools about which he can be excited and enthusiastic. These need to be good fits, not just also-rans. Spend time finding them.

Unfortunately, as more and more children apply to private schools, many of them have become significantly more selective than they were even two or three years ago. Don't forget that your child's visit and application, about which we'll talk at length in the next chapter, can strengthen his candidacy but won't make him an A student if he isn't one.

Safeties

Your safety schools need to be realistic; otherwise you face the possibility of having no choices. That could be painful for you and your child, especially if you are adamant about not staying in the public school system. Some families are fortunate enough to have excellent public schools and are only interested in leaving the neighborhood school if they can go to a specific private school. They are comfortable applying only to that school and understand that if their child does not get in, she will return to the public school.

Again, these are individual family decisions that depend on a host of circumstances. No matter what your specific situation, it is important to think about how you communicate your hopes and plans to your child. If you're adamant about not sending your child to a public school, then be careful about selecting some safety schools. Given the increasingly competitive nature of private school acceptance, it might be wise to keep your critique of your public schools to a minimum. Your child should understand why you would prefer to have him go to a private school, but if it works out that he doesn't get in to the ones you choose, it will be easier for him to return to the public school if you haven't spent hours pointing out its defects.

School admission is often the first time your child is judged on his merits by people who don't know your child or family. Although your youngster may have tried out for a traveling soccer team, chess league, or area-wide chorus, such evaluations tend to be specific. Children—and their parents—can understand that they might not be good enough at something to qualify for a select team or group. But we feel school admissions judge a child more broadly, looking at his academic performance, personal attributes, and teacher recommendations. And so much is beyond a parent's loving control. How will my child respond in an interview? What do the teachers really think about my child in comparison to other students? How does my child measure up? Most of us faced this as 17- and 18-year-olds, when we applied to college.

Families encountering the admissions process for the first time can feel a lot of stress from the many unknowns. Some families, worried that their child will be rejected, reassure him constantly, sending mixed signals and creating questions in the child's mind about how qualified his parents really think he is. Other families become consumed with the process and speculate and talk about it endlessly: Which of the four is the best choice? What are the odds of getting in? What is each school really looking for? Children in these situations often feel tremendous pressure to perform, to do those things that will improve their chances of acceptance. Some are urged to run for student government, even if they aren't interested, others are urged to question a teacher's grade or encouraged to play a sport they are neither interested in nor good at. Middle school children can react to this stress in many different ways. Some push themselves harder and harder to do more and more. Some become overwhelmed by the whole process and end up feeling detached and distant from their families, worried that they will disappoint their parents and teachers.

If your child doesn't get accepted to a private school, it will be easier for him to return to his old public school if you haven't spent hours pointing out its defects.

As a parent, try to monitor yourself carefully in the admissions process. Talk about the school search process with your spouse or friends when you are out of earshot of your child. While he may not express it openly, your child is likely to feel like he's on trial and will certainly fear being rejected. Remember that most middle school children are already self-critical and self-conscious. They are certain that someone will discover how inadequate they think they are. While they may seem confident to you, many are worried about admission and fear disappointing their parents.

Many kids worry that somehow it's not who they are that their parents love but rather what honors and prizes they have won. It makes them nervous to hear their parents talk constantly about their latest accomplishments. They read their parents' public pride as pressure to continue to do things and win prizes about which their parents can talk. Parents need to be mindful of the ways in which they can unintentionally increase that pressure.

If you're limited geographically, there may only be two or three schools that are possibilities. In some ways this makes for a more manageable but also more nervewracking search. If you're looking at boarding schools all over the country, you'll probably struggle to limit your list to about six schools, including reaches, targets, and safeties.

Sometimes it can be difficult to predict your child's chances of acceptance and therefore a little scary to limit your choices to only six or seven schools. You will have to be as realistic as possible, particularly when you determine her one or two safety schools. In choosing these schools, you want to be selective but realistic. Don't just slap two schools on to your list, hoping that your child will be accepted to several of her other choices. In a best-case scenario, your child will have several acceptances from which to choose. Realistically (and especially in today's competitive market) your child may be choosing only among her safety schools. Given that possibility, you and your child want to pick those schools as carefully as you pick her reach schools.

As you and your child narrow down your list to about six or seven schools, keep reminding yourself that you are looking for fit. The goal of a private school search is to find schools where your child will feel comfortable, will be challenged, and has a strong chance of being successful.

If, after reading and talking about each of the schools on your short list, you're feeling unsure or ambivalent about one or more of the schools, you might want to either expand your short list or identify some back-ups. The next stage is to visit these schools, if possible, and then, based on those visits, decide if your child should apply.

VISITING SCHOOLS

Even though the visiting process is stressful, try to enjoy it and to make it as enjoyable as you can for your child. He will, no doubt, be nervous and quick to pick up on any anxiety you reveal. Remind him of his many terrific qualities and aptitudes. Remind him of the things he does well and why you are so proud of him. Remind him that although the schools are looking at him, that you are also looking at these schools.

Try to let him take the lead in the visit as much as possible. Each child's role will vary tremendously depending on his own social skills and how involved he is in this search. It will be helpful if you can make it clear to everyone else that you are looking for a school that will be a good fit for him—not for you. If the school really fits him, it should meet your wishes for him, too.

Visits are arranged differently at each school. Some design individually tailored schedules so your child will get a chance to visit classes in which he indicated an interest (e.g., English, photography, astronomy, orchestra). He may meet with the head of the upper school or class dean for 15 to 20 minutes or with an athletic director or music director. In this scenario, he will have a number of guides, perhaps of different ages. He will have a host for lunch who will try to include him in a discussion with other students.

It's impossible to tell if a school will be a good fit until you visit it.

Other schools have the visiting student follow a current student's schedule for the day. The admissions office chooses an outgoing student who has volunteered to serve as a host and who has interests similar to your child's. Sometimes these visits lead to friendships; other times they can wear thin by third period. In either case, let the admissions office know candidly how the visit went. They want all visiting students and parents to have a good impression of their school and need to know if the host was gracious, knowledgeable, and positive. The guide may be a good kid but not right for this responsibility or it may be that a quiet student becomes a surprisingly amiable host.

INTERVIEWS

At most day schools, student interviews generally occur on the same day the student visits, without the parent present in the room. Interviews typically last 20 to 30 minutes and are either with an admissions officer, a teacher who sits on the admissions committee, or the principal. Interviewers tend to be personable, and often they are current or former teachers who are skilled at putting young people at ease.

Some quiet youngsters speak nonstop, and other more talkative youngsters speak in limited sentences. Whatever occurs in the interview, if your child seems uneasy about it, reassure him that the admissions representative understands that interviewees are nervous. Assure your child that the interview will not determine if he is accepted or not. It is only one of many ways the school is trying to get to know him.

Be sure to explain to your child that the interview is a chance to exchange views and address questions. If the visit occurs before you've sent in your application, the interviewer will often ask questions that appear on this form. If the interviewer has already received your child's application, he will often use it as a way to get your child to start talking. The interviewer is listening to ideas and words, but he is also trying to get some sense of who your child is.

Your child might feel more confident if you practice the interview at home. If she is willing, you might practice a firm handshake, clear eye contact, and answering simple questions. But if she refuses to practice with you, don't force her. It may be practicing with you rather than the idea of practicing that she is resisting. Remember, she may be worried about this process and that she might disappoint you. You might ask your child if there is someone else she would like to practice with—a relative or family friend. I would discourage asking a teacher at your current school if you sense any resentment about your decision to look for another school.

Assure your child that the interview will not determine if he is accepted or not. It is only one of many ways the school is trying to get to know him.

Urge your child to be herself. You might suggest she make a list of questions she'd like to ask the interviewer. Admissions officers enjoy answering a student's questions because it helps them get to know each child. If even after all this thought and practice, what do you do if your child feels she has blown the interview? Most likely, she did just fine. Most visits go extremely well, and your child probably made a favorable impression on the interviewer, her host, and the classroom teachers. She probably participated in class discussions when he felt comfortable, was included in a group project, and was involved in lunchroom discussions. But if your child had an unhappy experience or was getting ill, let the school know through either a call or note. Again, it wants the visit to be a successful experience for your child, and it might suggest another visit or an interview at a later date.

I would not suggest visiting a school if you and your child have no intention of enrolling there and if it will involve travelling a long distance to get there. That's not a good use of your time or the school's. But I also wouldn't hesitate to include a day school about which you don't know a great deal or have ambivalent feelings about, particularly if there aren't many schools in your area from which to choose. You may like the school a great deal; you will certainly learn more about the school, which may help you better understand other area schools. Acceptance at all private schools has become increasingly competitive, so it's important to look at several options.

Schedule your appointments carefully. Unless there is an emergency, don't change them. It's inconvenient for the school, and you may not be able to find another time that works. If your child is sick, don't go. Call the school as soon as it's clear that he won't be able to go. It's much better to cancel than to spend the entire visit worrying about your child, how he feels, and the impression he is making.

Decide ahead of time what type of clothing your child will wear for her visit and make it clear to her. Neither of you need the added stress of arguing about clothes the morning of your visit. It might be smart to have your child dress like the children she'll be visiting. If they wear a uniform, she'll be most comfortable dressing conservatively. If the boys wear jackets and ties, so will most visitors. Teenage visitors are self-conscious enough without needing to think everyone is staring at them. This is something you can ask the admissions officer about when you set up your appointment.

Visiting Schools in a New Town

If your school search involves a day school in another part of the country, you'll probably be trying to intersperse school visits with tours with a real estate agent. In the best-case scenario, you'll be able to schedule visits to several schools within a two- or three-day period. Seeing one school right after another may be tiring, but in some ways it encourages comparison. If possible, try to spend a couple of hours on each campus so by the time you get home, you'll have a real sense of each school. It may not be practical to schedule a return visit, although some families return for a second visit after their child has been accepted and they have narrowed down their choices to two or three. Distance and expense may preclude an additional visit, so it's important to make the most of the time you spend at each campus.

The natural anxiety and stress involved in relocating one's family can make school visits in a new town difficult for everyone. Some children are understandably angry or upset about moving; one parent may still not know what he or she will be doing professionally; and all of you might realize that the schools you're visiting are highly competitive.

A Written Checklist For Visits

Given this kind of tension, it will be helpful to design a written checklist to guide your visit and focus your observations. You and your child could work on a list together, or it might be more productive for you to make your own and to encourage your child to create her own. Some families have enjoyed making duplicates of the same list for each person to record his or her own opinions of the school. After each visit, they check off and rate each item and then compare their rankings. When you're visiting several schools, a written list makes it easier to keep each school straight in your mind and later to compare them all more accurately.

Having a list of things to evaluate and consider may force both parents and children to stop focusing on one aspect of the visit and to look at other facets of the school.

Just creating the list makes you and your child focus on the things about these schools that matter to you. What do you hope to learn by visiting? How will you be able to compare one school with another? How will you know whether to apply to a school or not? A predetermined list also makes it easier to escape judging the entire school by the tour guide. He's cute; your daughter wants to go there. He's a computer whiz; she refuses to consider it. A particularly pleasant or unpleasant conversation, a class, or a snafu can unfairly color the entire visit. Having a list of things to evaluate and consider may force both parents and children to stop focusing on one aspect of the visit to look at other facets of the school.

By its nature, day-to-day life in any school is always slightly unpredictable and perhaps because of that spontaneity, stimulating. It's not unusual for the admissions officers to not know that a class is on a field trip, that the tour guide has to take a make-up test, or that there's an

1. Rank from 1 (terrible) to 5 (great):
   The campus _____/Athletic Fields _____/Dorms _____/Dining Room _____/
   Classrooms _____/Computer Labs _____ (or Theater, Photo Lab or whatever would
   be of special interest.

   The best facility: _____

   The worst facility: _____

2. The kids seemed

	Yes	No
To work hard	___	___
Smart	___	___
Friendly	___	___
Weird	___	___
Like me	___	___
Happy	___	___
Bored	___	___

3. The teachers seemed

Friendly	___	___
Interested in their students	___	___
Interested in me	___	___
Hard	___	___
Smart	___	___
Easy to talk to	___	___

4. The work seemed

Like my work	___	___
Harder	___	___
Easier	___	___
More interesting	___	___

5. The classes or activities I would want to take are:

6. Things I didn't like:

7. Things I forgot to find out:

unexpected assembly. Experienced admissions folks will hastily regroup and whenever possible, find other ways to accommodate your child's interests. This is easier for them to do if they know before your visit of any special interests you or your child has.

Your List

Although as parents you could certainly share the same list and end up with lots to talk about, you'll probably also want to focus on the financial questions and the more subjective issues about whether you will feel comfortable entrusting your child into the hands of these strangers. We'll spend a lot of time talking about the financial issues in Chapter 7, but this seems like an appropriate place to talk a little bit about how to get your hands around these more subjective issues.

It's impossible to tell whether a school is going to feel like a right fit until you visit it. Although the factual data is important, most parents want to see how that one faculty member relates to every ten students (as advertised in the catalog: "1:10 faculty-student ratio") rather than just know he's there, has a master's degree, and coaches one sport. You want to walk down the halls and hear how those students ("60 percent of whom have 600 or higher SAT verbal scores") talk to each other and to their teachers. You'll want to hear whether those kids (8 percent of whom take AP exams or go to the University of Wherever) laugh, enjoy their work, and are proud of their school. You'll want to see whether the kids all look alike, whether the classrooms seem inviting, whether everyone looks horribly stressed or bored. Do people speak to each other in the halls? Do the bulletin boards advertise interesting projects and activities?

What posters are on the walls? Is there student art in the halls? And does the artwork look as though the art department is encouraging each student to explore his own style?

Most schools are eager to display student work; you can learn a lot by seeing what is posted, its quality, and the variety. How well do the students write? Do you only see the work of a few students being posted and celebrated? As you pass by computer and science labs, try to get a sense of how much they are used and by whom. Many schools boast about the number of computers, but it is important to see if they are actually used to enhance student learning or are just for window dressing.

You'll also get a pretty good sense of the diversity of the community and whether diversity is merely tolerated or actually celebrated. Is the faculty as diverse as the student body? Do you see students and teachers working together outside of classrooms? Do the kids seem to be working and engaged, or does it feel like a lot of kids are just hanging around?

The list could go on and on, but at the end of a visit what you want to feel is that your child could be comfortable, would be cared for, and would be encouraged and stretched to maximize her potential.

You want to leave the campus feeling that the school learned just as much about you and your child as you and your child learned about the school.

The Parent Interview

Although your interview will not be as structured as your child's, your visit to each campus will include opportunities for you to talk with someone in the admissions office. The most satisfying and informative visits usually include some less formal conversations with students and teachers. Think

Approach the
parent interview as
a chance to share
your sense of your
child, his strengths,
and your concerns
and dreams for him.
You don't need to
share every detail,
but don't omit any
significant
information about
your child's
schooling, his
learning style, and
family.

about each school before you visit. Do your homework carefully so you'll be able to make the most of the time you spend there.

The school will want to know why you're interested in it. With some thought, you should be able to explain reasons other than your dissatisfaction with your current school. It will be helpful to share your initial impressions of the school to see if the admissions staff feels that you've gotten an accurate sense of the place from the catalogs and brochures.

Also be sure to ask your questions. Ask about the math program or whether a Jewish student will feel comfortable there. If it's a boarding school, ask about weekend activities. What is the school's policy on drugs? You want to leave the campus feeling that the school learned a fair amount about you and your child and that you and your child learned just as much about the school.

Visiting schools can be a lot of fun and can give parents an all-too-rare opportunity to spend time with just one of your children. It's fun to hear what they think and to see each school through their eyes. No matter how strong your reactions to each school, curb your tongue until you've given your child a chance to share his opinions and observations. Too many adolescents get caught up in reacting to their parents' views, either positively or negatively, and never share or fully develop their own thoughts. Some kids may be in a negative stage, so that no matter what view their parents take, they take the opposite. Other children, especially when they are nervous about the whole search process, will quickly agree with their parents' views despite their own misgivings or initial reactions. Remember, it's your child who will be going to one of these schools, so it's important that he be encouraged to express and share his reactions to each school. You'll probably find that he'll notice lots of things that you overlooked.

Some kids are not eager to talk about their visit in detail. For some, it's important to process it for themselves before they describe it to you. For others, it's all too threatening, too unnerving. Try not to grill your child. Wait and listen carefully. It may be that she'll share more with a sibling or close friend. Two or three days later, you may learn more. Urge her to fill in her reaction list. She doesn't have to share this with anyone now, but it will help her keep the various schools straight when she wants to compare them.

Many families enjoy it when both parents can visit each school with their child. However, sometimes both parents aren't able to take that much time off from work. The child and parent who did visit should share their experiences with the parent who couldn't come. This situation might also inspire you and your child to make more extensive use of your checklists.

Enjoy your visits. Learn a lot. Take some notes. And when you get home, we'll be ready to start filling out those dreaded applications.

Short List of Schools

1. Reach School—Hard data would suggest that your child has only an outside chance of being accepted.
2. Another Reach School
3. Target School—Hard data would suggest that your child is within the school's acceptable range.
4. Another Target School
5. Safety School—Hard data would suggest that your child would be considered a strong candidate.
6. Another Safety School

The Applications

After you have visited several schools and have narrowed your choices down to a reasonably short list that includes reaches, targets, and safeties, you are ready to begin the application process. Schools usually revise and update their admissions materials over the summer, so call in late August or early September to ask for their new catalogs, application materials, current publications, and most recent college acceptance lists. Some schools will ask you to fill out a preliminary application form before they schedule an interview or send you the full application. Although these preliminary application forms are usually fairly short and simple, it might be smart to make a duplicate to use as a working draft. Remember that this will become a part of your child's file, and you want it to reflect well on both of you. Fill it out carefully and return it in a timely fashion to allow you and the school plenty of time to process the regular application. Given today's increasingly competitive market, deadlines are critical. Many schools have become less willing to consider last-minute, after-the-deadline applications, and most have little, if any, financial aid left for students who apply late.

You will want your child's application to be clean, neat, and carefully prepared, so make a duplicate copy of each application to use as a working draft and file the original away until you are ready to fill it out. Also, put together a check list for each of the schools to which your child is applying. It should include each step tht is required by the school and a place to indicate when you completed it. Although the specifics will vary with each school, your list might look something like this:

Next Steps for Heaven School	Done	Date
Complete and send in the preliminary application form		
Call the admissions office to arrange an interview		
Complete and send in application with parent signature and application fee		
Complete and send in student application		
Sign and send transcript request form (to current school)		
Give recommendation forms and stamped envelopes to teachers (list names of teachers)		
Give recommendation forms and stamped envelopes to others (list names)		
Arrange to take SSAT or ISEE, preferably on November or December dates		
If applicable, request financial aid forms		

Each application is different, and you may find it helpful to review the samples in the Appendix of this book. You should also take a look at the Common Application developed by nine California high schools. This joint project is modeled on the Common Application used by more than thirty colleges. We expect to see more of these developed in urban areas with numerous private schools.

APPLICATION ESSAYS

Parent and student essays are important to the admissions committee, which is eager to know more about why you have selected its school. The committee wants to see if the school's philosophy will resonate with your hopes for your child. Although some parents may be as nervous about answering their questions as their children are about completing theirs, look at this as a chance to talk about what you value and why you think this school should be a good fit for your child.

Parent Essays

Most parents want small classes, excellent college guidance, strong athletic programs, and broad arts offerings. You will want to try to personalize these general statements so they relate to your child and your hopes for her. For example, you might want to talk about how small classes could enhance your child's learning. Perhaps your child is looking for a larger, equally talented peer group than is in her current class. Is your child a good athlete who would benefit from playing with older and stronger players? Or maybe you think your child would benefit from a postgraduate program because she started school young and may need to take an additional year before starting college.

Take a look at some real-life examples. They have been altered to conceal the identities of the writers.

In response to the typical question "Why are you interested in this school for your child?", one parent writes:

"Because of Harry's auditory processing weaknesses (he is a visual learner), we believe he would benefit significantly from the smaller class sizes offered by this school. We also firmly believe that a

smaller school will give Harry a better chance to expand his activities and horizons beyond his schoolwork and sports to include participation in clubs, school plays, and civic activities that are unavailable to him in his current school because of its size. Finally, the environment of motivated students who want to attend top universities and involved parents who know the importance of a premium, top-quality secondary education will reinforce Harry's own work ethic and his and our own shared emphasis on education."

Responding to the same question, another astute parent writes:

"Sara is the third of three daughters, and her older sisters both attended public schools. In both cases, Sparrow County schools were quite satisfactory. However, as the years have passed and as Sara has developed, our experience with the local school system has changed. Sara is a child who possesses tremendous talent and drive, but for a variety of reasons, these qualities are not being stimulated in her current school. Although her recent grades have been fairly good, overall she has not really tapped her true capabilities. It is for this reason that we are looking to a private school to help challenge and motivate her academically."

Candor

Be realistic and truthful in your application. Some parents worry that if they reveal their concerns about their child's social or academic difficulties, this will hurt him in a competitive process. That may or may not be the case because there certainly are circumstances in which a school will feel it is not a good match for a student with special needs. However, not revealing a learning evaluation, serious disciplinary problems, or psychological counseling your child has had is misleading and could cause a committee to turn down your child when the information comes out in the teacher recommendations or school transcript. I'm not suggesting that you document every little stumble your child may have made, but it would be foolish not to share any significant event or insight into his learning style.

Schools expect kids to make mistakes and have difficulties—it's a part of growing and learning. They also believe that parents, students, and teachers need to be honest, open partners. If information is withheld in the admissions process, the school worries that a parent will not be open and honest once the child is enrolled. No admissions officer assumes that a child will automatically continue to have the same difficulties he had in his former school, but they want to have a complete, candid picture of your child and his past experience. If parents haven't revealed what steps had been taken in the past to help their child, valuable time can be lost figuring out how to support a new student.

The best use of prior troubles occurs when parents are confident enough to reveal a difficulty and ask how a particular school might handle a situation. This way, the parent can gain both the admissions officer's respect and some useful information. For example, your daughter may have had social problems two years ago and been suspended once for cutting class. You will probably be more comfortable discussing this kind of problem if you feel it has been resolved, but you might bring up her behavior to learn more about the school's philosophy and disciplinary approaches. In the meantime, you have shared something that the admissions committee will, in all likelihood, learn about from your daughter's teacher recommendations or school transcript.

Although the essay form might seem intimidating, you are not writing an essay to be graded by the English department.

Here is how one parent revealed a difficulty that her son had experienced and put it in a context that would not alarm the admissions committee:

"Jason is a fast learner and can become impatient and easily bored. Restless eighth-grade boys are probably every teacher's worst nightmare. Although occasionally Jason's restlessness was annoying to his math teacher, his English teacher was terrific at channeling his energy into additional projects. I'm confident that your curriculum is so much more demanding than..."

Or perhaps your child had a learning evaluation when he was ten because both you and the school were concerned about his rate of reading. Through tutoring, he has improved, but you are wondering about the school's stance on untimed tests. What accommodations are teachers willing to make? In addition to sharing an open assessment of your son's strengths and weaknesses, you are showing the school that you know your child, that you are looking for the right fit for him, and that you will be an agreeable partner should he need extra support. From the school's perspective, this bodes well for a good working relationship.

Above all, be yourself. Write in your own style with your own words. Be truthful about why the school appeals to you and what you hope your child will learn there. Don't just say what you think the school wants to hear. The admissions committee wants to get to know you and your values. Although the form might seem intimidating, you are not writing an essay to be graded by the English department. This is a chance to share your hopes and dreams for your child and to explain why you think this particular school would be a good fit for him.

Let me share with you a few other excerpts from parents who realized that these applications are an important opportunity to give the admissions committee real insight into their children:

"Last year, Jeff's father was diagnosed with cancer; he died earlier this year. This affected Jeff's interest in extracurricular activities at school. He became quite withdrawn and seemed to focus inward, spending more time writing. I guess he was more comfortable expressing his pain and sorrow in written form than in conversation. He has matured tremendously this past year."

And this:

"Your school seems to foster an acceptance and tolerance of others with different interests, and students are not stereotyped by the group they hang out with. This will be a great relief to Robin, who unfortunately is in a school where the smart kids are labeled nerds *and either ridiculed or ignored by the* in *group."*

Student Essays

Your child will be asked to answer several questions that relate to his activities, favorite academic subjects, and summer experiences. In short paragraphs, each child is usually asked to respond to several questions, ranging from "Who has influenced you the most and why?" to "What is your favorite book and why?" to "What do you hope to gain by coming to this school?" Many schools require both short responses and a few longer essays, often two or three 1-page responses. In addition, many require each candidate to send a graded copy of a recent piece of work, such as an English composition, a history research paper, or a science lab. They are interested in seeing what your child is producing in his current classes.

What are schools looking for in these essays? In your statement, they look for your understanding of your child and why you think she belongs at that school. In her writing, they're looking for how your child defines herself, her interests, her expectations, and her voice. How well does the student express herself? What vocabulary does she select? Does she have a clear interest that the school can foster and nurture?

Applications should be neatly completed and proofread. Spend time talking through the questions before your child begins filling it out. Discuss ideas, jot down notes, and draw out from your child what he hopes will happen by switching schools. Remember to let him use his own words and avoid editing his work as much as you possibly can. You'll have your chance; this is his chance. However, it does make sense to read over his statements and point out any misspellings or incomplete thoughts before he copies them on to the application. Needless to say, depending on their nature, ability, and training, some eighth graders can produce sophisticated writing pieces while others write in a choppy, immature style. It would be impossible to classify any essay as "typical" of an average ninth grade applicant because different schools attract widely diverse applicant pools. Some bright eighth graders have not yet learned to express themselves effectively while others are extremely articulate. We have selected a range of essays, with any names and specific references removed to protect the identities of the writers, to give you some sense of how some eighth graders present themselves.

Although a few middle schoolers are gifted writers or blessed with the ability to be truly original, most kids would do best to answer the questions directly and not be tempted to craft what could be received as "too clever" or

Many schools require candidates to send a graded copy of a recent piece of work, such as an English composition, history research paper, or science lab.

"simply bizarre." Admissions committees do not expect to read six pages of rhymed couplets as an answer to why your child wants to go to their school, nor do they want to read detailed biographical sketches of Einstein or Thomas Jefferson in response to a question about someone your child admires.

They expect to read about siblings, summers at camp, grandparents, and Little League coaches. They are interested in hearing about family trips to amusement parks and why your daughter liked *To Kill A Mockingbird* or cried all the way through *Of Mice And Men*. Encourage your child to write about the things she knows and likes. Certainly you want her to write in organized, coherent sentences and paragraphs, but help her avoid a stilted essay that is full of a lot of words she copied out of a dictionary.

Let me share some examples that range from the fairly straightforward, simple approach to some quite sophisticated thinking.

My Favorite Character

1. "During the course of eighth grade, I read *A Tree Grows in Brooklyn*, a novel which had been assigned to us (my class) by our English teacher. I found its topic to be so realistic and the characters to be easy to understand and relate to. One character in particular who stuck out in my mind was Sissy, the aunt of the main character.

    Despite the fact that Sissy was the most provocative character in the book, she was also one of the most kind and generous. *A Tree Grows in Brooklyn* was set during the First World War and also during a conservative era (at least by our standards) where you had to work for everything you earned. The author brought the harsh realities of the time to life and used Sissy to make the setting a little more bearable for the reader.

She became my favorite character not only because she added relief to a hard time in her life and her family's, but also because she had all the characteristics I strive for. Although she lived a somewhat questionable lifestyle, she never cared what anyone thought of her! Sissy was kind to everyone, and you could always count on her."

2. "I am doing this essay on Gollum, a character in J.R.R. Tolkien's *The Hobbit* and *The Lord of the Rings*. Gollum is an evil character, but I think he is one of my favorite characters in the books, because he has such a personality. I would love to meet him if he were a real person. He is a lonely character and sometimes I feel sorry for him. He also tends to talk to himself, and one of my favorite lines of his is, 'What has it got in it's pockets's?'. The fact that he always adds 'S's' gives him that snake like quality, which is funny. He is cut off from the world and has almost no experience in talking. I think he is sneaky and tricky. He always has a trick up his sleeve."

Write about an activity you enjoy.

1. "I have been riding horses since I was very young. I have fond memories of every Sunday driving forty-five minutes to the barn to ride for the day. My

sisters would go through their regular riding routine, and then it would be my turn. I started slowly, with both my sisters holding me on from both sides, and my dad walking the horse with a lead line. Then one sister wouldn't be on one side, and my dad would keep walking me around. Pretty soon, my dad would walk around beside me with the lead line off the horse and no one to hold me on, and I would steer for myself. As I got older, I learned to walk by myself, steer better, to trot, and finally to a canter with no help. My sisters both grew out of the horse phase but I am still enjoying horses as much as I did on my first ride."

Who is a person you admire and/or who has influenced you most? Why?

1. "One person I admire is my best friend, Tom. Birth complications left him with a scarred face. He never uses his problem to get pity from others nor as an excuse for not being able to do something. In fact, he has great courage and will try anything."

2. "A person I admire is my grandfather, Phil A. Smith, who recently died. I feel that he was an inspirational person. He showed determination and drive when he became a Deputy Chief of the NYPD. I think those are two admirable traits."

3. "The person I admire most is my science teacher, Michelle Smith. Not only is she my best teacher, she's my friend. Everyday she extends herself beyond the call of duty. She's involved in saving our planet.

Last year she took thirty of her students, me included, to the Student Summit at Sandy Hook. She helped us conduct all types of tests, which taught me a lot. She's showed me my duties to my environment."

What currently interests you most (in or out of school)?

1. "In school I am interested in math and science. I enjoy math because it is something that makes my mind work and doing math work is something I take great pride in. I enjoy science because my science teacher does everything hands on. This way I can understand something by seeing it with my own eyes."

2. "Five times a week, my mother drives me to the cold, empty ice rink. I yawn as I tie up my skates, until they are tight enough to support my feet. I open the door and enter the deserted ice rink with a smile. At this moment, I realize why I love and adore this sport with all my heart.

   Figure skating has taught me how to be patient with myself. In this sport, I have to count on myself and only myself. If I mess up I can't blame someone or something for my mistake. I had to learn this in order to become a better skater, mentally. When I am having a hard time while practicing, I have to remember that everyone has trouble in one form or another at least one time in their skating experience. Most importantly, it has taught me that in order to achieve excellence, you have to work hard consistently."

Parent Help

The application process can provide a springboard for wonderful discussions, but it can also become a point of tension. Any well-intentioned editing suggestions can be inferred by a sensitive youngster as harsh criticism. Somehow, he thinks that you are saying that he cannot make it on his own merits. Remember, too, that your child will be completing an in-house essay for each school, usually on the day he visits or during standardized testing. If you are too heavily involved in shaping and editing the essays he wrote on the application, these are going to be in stark contrast to the one he will write by himself at school.

It is often helpful to allow considerable time to revise the essay-writing portion of the application. Both you and your child could write a first draft and then let it sit for four or five days. Take another look at both the parent and student essays before you copy them on to the formal application. This is the time to amend or delete.

More is not necessarily better. Admissions committees will be reading hundreds of applications, so you want to make your points clearly and succinctly. Anxious, nervous parents have been known to produce ten-page descriptions of their extraordinary 13-year-old child. Other equally well-intentioned parents have presented admissions committees with huge photojournalist family albums and elaborate collections of their child's art work from age 3 on. While an admissions officer understands that parents are only trying to present their child in the best light, there is a lot to be said for moderation. Admissions officers worry that if parents seem overbearing or unreasonable in the admissions office, they will be just as difficult if they became members of the community.

> **More is not necessarily better. Admissions committees will be reading hundreds of applications, so you want to make your points clearly and succinctly.**

If you visited the campus and had an interview before the application due date, you might use your observations of the campus to help you craft a statement that reflects your visit. You probably have a clearer sense of what this particular school can provide for your child and what your child might contribute to enhance the school. It might be effective in your essay to refer to that visit and to your impressions of the school. If your visit can't take place until after the application deadline, this can just as easily be turned to your advantage. Having completed the application before your interview can help crystallize your thinking and allow you to reflect in the interview on your expectations and perceptions of the school and how it might fit your child.

ACTIVITIES

In addition to the essays, each application will include questions about your child's interests and activities. While it is tempting to pad a resume to make an applicant look more accomplished, resist the temptation. It's your first time to fill out these forms, but the admissions committee has seen thousands of applications. If the dedication to community service that you or your child mentioned prominently on page 1 really occurred only four times, and then with a youth group, that will eventually become clear in some other part of the process. If it's an interest that you hope your child will pursue at this particular school, say so and leave it at that. If your child is an avid reader and has taken four years of piano, it is better to list those. Keep in mind that schools are generally looking for the genuine article—children who have a good sense of themselves, and parents who know their children. Schools are also concerned about over-scheduled, overcommitted students. They worry about children whose applications include long lists of activities, clubs, and interests. Questions often come up about balance and a child's ability to manage an increased workload and so many outside activities.

RECOMMENDATIONS

As private school admissions have become increasingly competitive, more parents have started asking friends, relatives, teachers, and coaches to write recommendations for their child. This is tricky ground. Experienced college admissions officers have been known to comment that the "thicker the folder, the thicker the kid." Translated: if a student's application includes lots of unsolicited letters touting her "wonderful" attributes, the admissions committee starts to wonder why she would need all these letters if she is so "wonderful."

It may be that there are one or two people whose input was not solicited in the application process who know your child well and who are willing to write on her behalf. Don't ask someone who knows you but not your child to write a recommendation. His opinion of you will not mean much to the admissions committee.

Having your child's soccer coach, girl scout leader, or music teacher write a letter that outlines some of your child's best features might be a good idea. These letters are most helpful when they include specific examples of your child's personality, perhaps her tenacity, work ethic, or leadership potential. In rare but extremely fortuitous situations, you may know someone who knows your child *and* the particular school to which she's applying. The admissions committee will be interested to hear from someone who can address the question of whether your child seems like a good fit for this school.

Don't ask someone who knows you but not your child for a recommendation. His opinion of you will not mean much to the admissions committee.

Don't despair if you do not have such a contact. Most applicants don't. If you're fortunate enough to have many such contacts, be careful not to overplay this card. Any admissions committee can get turned off if the members feel they are being bombarded. One or two letters from people who know your child well will be the most helpful.

Most schools consider their recommendations to be confidential and ask teachers and others to mail their comments directly to the school. You or your child should ask each person if he will write a reference letter and give him the appropriate forms and stamped envelopes addressed to each school. Be sure to tell them the deadlines and give them plenty of time to complete the forms.

If you are asking someone to write to more than one school, you might suggest that they write one letter and use a copy of it for each school. Most schools are perfectly happy to receive a xeroxed copy of a letter attached to their form. If you have asked someone to write a reference because he knows your child and the specific school to which he is applying, he should write a specific letter about your child and that school.

DEADLINES

Most schools ask that the parent and student essays, all teacher recommendations, and the school transcripts be in the admissions office by mid-January. This deadline works well for both the student's family as well as the school because it allows enough time to make sure all the pieces are collected. The admissions office will review your child's file to make sure all the required materials are in and will alert you if a teacher recommendation has not yet been received or if a transcript does not include the most recent grades. Usually, completed application files are reviewed by admissions committees by mid-February.

Although the interview is an important part of the application process, scheduling conflicts or just the sheer number of applicants at a particular school may prevent you and your child from having your interview by the time of the application deadline. Do not worry—the visits are an essential part of the process, but your child's chances will not be hurt if you have to have a late-February visit. Most admissions committees need to work until the last deadline prioritizing candidates and waiting to make final decisions for children whose interviews have already been scheduled but have not happened yet. Some schools offer families who would need to travel a long distance to visit the school the option of having an interview with an alumni or former teacher of the school who can meet them closer to their home. If you are unable to visit the school, be sure to take advantage of this opportunity to both learn more about the school and to give someone associated with the school a chance to see what your child might contribute.

Most private schools in the same region agree to share a common date for mailing decision letters and not to require parents to return their contracts before an agreed-upon date. This agreement is intended to allow each candidate to hear from all the schools to which he has applied before he has to accept any offer. Letters in many areas are mailed March 1 or March 10, with contracts due back about one month later. Unfortunately, some schools will sometimes send their letters earlier than your area's agreed-upon date and ask you for an early response. You have every right to hear from each school first and to wait until the contract deadline to respond to each one.

Rolling Admissions

Your child may be applying to a school that has a policy of rolling admissions. This usually means that the school will consider candidates at any time of the year, and some schools will even allow students to join the school mid-year. This has certainly been helpful to families in which an unavoidable move or a crisis in their child's current school have made an immediate transfer desirable. But even in a rolling admissions situation, completing the entire application in a timely fashion could work to your advantage. Glitches do happen, recommendations occasionally get lost, or your current school may forget to send your child's latest grades. Don't waste time worrying about that possibility. Each school goes through each child's application file very carefully, and they will let you know if anything is missing.

Now What?

Your entire family can breathe a collective sigh of relief when the last application is stuffed in the last envelope and you can scratch off the last item on your To Do List. Now it's time to turn your attention to the issue that has probably been nagging you throughout this process: If your child is accepted, how in the world are you going to pay the tuition?

Financial Aid

Contrary to the stereotype, many private school families need and receive considerable financial aid. Independent schools are expensive choices in after-tax dollars. Nevertheless, increasing numbers of families are seeking an independent school education for their children and are willing to make enormous personal sacrifices and to assume long-term debt. Faced with regularly rising tuition, many parents are applying for and receiving tuition assistance in the form of scholarships, grants, and loans.

Each school has its own guidelines and philosophy, but there are some features of financial aid that are germane to most. Many schools award financial aid strictly on the basis of documented need (we'll talk in a minute about how that documentation is done), without regard to a student's academic or athletic merit. As long as your child is an acceptable student to the school, your family has financial need, and the school has enough money to give, you will be eligible to receive money. If your child is a star basketball player, but the official documentation shows that you can afford to pay the tuition, these schools will not give you money—no matter how much they want to see your daughter on their basketball court.

Boards of trustees of private schools wrestle endlessly with the need to raise additional monies to fund their financial aid programs. Some schools with large endowments operate much like colleges and are able to offer several million dollars in outright grants per year as well as help parents to arrange long-term loans. Most independent schools report that 15–20 percent of their students receive aid. Larger grants and the greater numbers of awards usually go to upper school students in a K–12 grade school.

No matter how large a school's endowment or how many students receive financial aid, there is never enough money to fund families to the full extent of their need or to enroll all the qualified candidates who apply. Each year, admissions officers agonize over the highly qualified candidates they lose when families are not offered enough aid to cover their financial need. In recent years most schools have found themselves accepting many highly qualified students who don't end up coming for financial reasons.

Most independent schools report that 15–20 percent of their students receive aid.

Schools are primarily educational organizations, but they must also make sound business decisions, which include balancing institutional needs against the desirability of a particular candidate. Schools with limited resources need to ask a series of questions in determining to whom they should offer financial aid: How long will the student be on assistance? Are the family's circumstances likely to improve over the course of the three or four years that the child attends? How large is the grant, and would it be better to enroll two students with smaller grants than to provide all this money to one student? Are there grandparents who could help with their grandchild's tuition? Does the family live within its means or is it willing to cut back to cover the partial tuition costs asked of them? Will this family fail to live up to its part of the tuition agreement, becoming a bad debt and putting the school in the position of having to ask a terrific student to leave midway through his career at the school? Does the family have hidden assets that could be sold to defray costs?

These are difficult questions to ask, but financial aid committees or officers must ask them as they assess each family's ability to pay. Better to ask hard questions and have difficult discussions in the early stages of the process rather than to interrupt an education after families have overextended themselves to make the dream come true for their child.

WHO SHOULD APPLY FOR FINANCIAL AID?

By all means, apply for financial aid if you believe you might qualify. You have nothing to lose other than the time it will take to fill out the paperwork. Even families with large incomes may qualify because each situation is unique. Families from a wide range of socioeconomic strata receive aid. Nearly all schools have need-blind admissions policies, which means that your child's application will be judged by his qualifications, not your ability to pay. His chances of admission will not be effected by whether you apply for aid. If your child is admitted and awarded aid, most schools will allow only a few individuals in the school to know that your child is receiving assistance because the information is held in the strictest confidence and not released to teachers, coaches, dorm parents, or parents of other students.

Unlike colleges, students on aid are not usually expected to perform work tasks around the school; therefore, unless a student tells his friends or teachers that he is receiving aid, neither the kids nor the adults in the community will know anything about your financial arrangements. Some schools provide a work option in which students are paid for on-campus jobs. If you are interested in this type of program, you will need to ask each school about its philosophy and specific program. Many students in schools all over the country choose to find high-paying summer jobs that will enable them to contribute to their families' educational expenses.

Need-Based Aid

Be aware that the process of applying for aid can feel intrusive and that you may feel inadequate or frustrated for being unable to provide a private school education as easily as others. You may find that this process stirs up feelings that you didn't know you had or makes you second-guess decisions made long ago. Keep in mind that this is a common reaction that is shared by many who go through this process. Some parents find themselves wishing they had opted for a different career or resenting the fact that their spouse had not struck it rich or had been passed over for a promotion. You can find yourself wondering how you will ever pay for your child's college education or for your next child's private school education. Many parents find themselves experiencing what might be described as the adult equivalent of their child's lament, "I'll never get into these schools. Why should I even bother to apply?" It's tempting to throw up your hands and opt out.

The process will feel judgmental, even though it is not intended to be. You will be asked to reveal your most intimate financial details—mortgage payments, vacation costs, credit card debt, make and year of car, investment plans, health costs, amount paid for outside activities, church or synagogue donations, charitable deductions, dinners out—and then asked to state what you can afford to pay toward tuition and why. Some schools ask you to write a letter

> Remember, admissions and financial aid staff members are usually a sympathetic audience, having made similar career choices and sacrifices to enroll their children in independent schools.

explaining any unusual or extenuating circumstances. The process can be daunting and humbling, but try to remember that the admissions officers are only asking for this information to make the best possible decision for their schools and their current families. Independent schools want families like yours and are actively looking for socioeconomic diversity as well as racial, ethnic, religious, and geographic diversity. As costs have increased in the last fifteen years, schools have openly worried about losing the middle class, particularly when there is more than one child in the family. Schools recognize that it would be to everyone's disadvantage if they ended up having only very wealthy and very poor students. Middle-income families, defined as earning gross incomes of $40,000 to $120,000, generally qualify for assistance. The amount of assistance awarded obviously depends on the particular school's tuition as well as your income, assets, and number of dependents.

PARENT'S FINANCIAL STATEMENT

Most private schools will ask you to complete an application supplied by the School and Student Service for Financial Aid (SSS), which is administered by the Educational Testing Service. More than 2,000 schools from across the country are members of SSS, which is by far the largest financial-need determination service at the secondary school level. Once a family has completed and returned this confidential statement of their finances, known as the Parents' Financial Statement (PFS), SSS provides each school with a preliminary estimate of how much that family could contribute toward educational expenses. Using an outside evaluation assures that all the schools to which you are applying will base their calculations on the same data. You can get a copy of the PFS from any school to which you apply, and you will only need to fill it out once.

Although SSS processes applications from December through July, schools are eager to get your data as soon as possible. Many request a copy of your PFS application when you mail it to SSS so the school can begin their preliminary calculations while it awaits the SSS analysis.

The underlying assumption of SSS is that parents have an obligation to pay for their children's education to the extent to which they are able. SSS defines financial aid as the difference between the cost of education and the expected family contribution. In determining how much money a particular family can pay, SSS considers family income, assets, liabilities, number and ages of the children, the expense of their education, age of the parents, and their provisions for retirement. SSS tries to treat each family fairly and the same, but it also recognizes that a family could have unusual circumstances that are beyond their control. It sees a critical distinction between family expenses that are by choice and those that are unavoidable.

Although all these factors are considered in this analysis, the most important component is family income. To the surprise of many, SSS recognizes that even families with an income of more than $100,000 might need financial aid to send their child to a private school. Many of these families have more than one child in a tuition-paying school and perhaps also face one or more college tuitions.

It takes between six and eight hours to complete the SSS application. Parents need to get their taxes done as early as possible and to write a cover letter pleading their case to SSS. Some private schools offer evening or weekend workshops to help families complete the forms. Take advantage of this opportunity if it is provided because you will learn tips that might help you enormously. If the school you are applying to does not offer sessions, read its financial aid material thoroughly and call the financial aid officers if you have any questions. They are there to help you—and, after all, they will be reading your application soon enough.

Most schools are eager to help with the process and will assign a particular person, sometimes in the admissions office and sometimes not, to answer any and all of your questions. Be sure to seek him out. Schools urge you to send in your financial aid applications in a timely manner because funds are limited and are quickly depleted after the initial awards have been made. Few schools have sufficiently large endowments to provide all the aid that their students need for which they qualify. Although there are occasions when grants are turned down by a student and therefore made available to another student late in the process, these cases are unusual. Don't hurt your chances for aid by turning in late or incomplete forms.

EVALUATE YOUR PRIORITIES

What the financial aid process offers all parents, whether they qualify for aid or not, is the chance to take a hard look at priorities and expenditures. That isn't always a lot of fun, but it certainly will help guide your child's college search in only a few years. What trade-offs are you willing to make?

- Are you willing to forgo vacations to put that money toward tuition?

- Can you afford to maintain one car for a longer period of time or choose a less expensive model if your old one needs to be replaced?

Be sure your child understands that a decision about financial aid is based on family income, not athletic prowess or academic achievement.

- In what ways can you cut back on entertainment, clothing costs, and luxury household items to make tuition payments?

- Are parents as fully employed as possible and in the fields in which they were trained?

- Would the money you would spend on tuition payments be better spent on mortgage payments in a district with a better public school system?

- At what point will you resent paying tuition rather than taking your family on a much-deserved vacation or making a necessary household repair?

- Would your children benefit more from music lessons, travel, and cultural activities than a private school education if it means these will have to be cut out to pay for tuition?

- Will your child benefit from the education but feel too much pressure to fit in or too much pressure to perform?

Consider these questions carefully and as realistically as possible. Sadly, many private school students live in fear of losing their financial aid because of a poor test grade or a terrible athletic season. Be sure your child understands that a decision about financial aid is based on family income, not athletic prowess or academic achievement. Most children realize that their family has made sacrifices to provide this opportunity for them and therefore are appropriately conscientious.

Unfortunately, some parents who have made enormous sacrifices to send their child to a particular school become unusually demanding and highly critical of the school and its programs that the teachers wonder why they continue to enroll their children. Often, and after a great number of discussions, these parents reveal that they examine everything against what they are sacrificing. Although we all assess the costs and benefits in many areas of our lives, the costs—both actual and personal—can become too great for some of these parents to see the positive aspects of their child's enrollment.

DIFFERENT SCHOOLS: DIFFERENT GRANTS

SSS does not determine how much financial aid a school will offer your child. Each school makes that decision independently. SSS merely analyzes your family's finances and determines what it thinks you could contribute to your child's education. For a multitude of reasons, you could complete your PFS, SSS could determine what you could contribute, and you still might get five substantially different financial aid offers from five different schools.

Schools reserve the right to offer you more or less aid than the SSS analysis might suggest. If School A's financial aid resources are limited and it has an enormous number of acceptable students who also qualify for aid, the school might decide to offer smaller grants to ten students than to offer large grants to the top three students. School B could look at your same financial data and decide that it is so eager to have your daughter attend that it will offer you as much aid as the SSS determined you needed. Grants become even harder to predict in schools that award financial aid to children they really want to come there, whether their families need aid or not.

Rest assured that however a school calculates the contributions of noncustodial parents or day-care or graduate school expenses, it does it the same way for every applicant. Your responsibilities are to fill out the PFS, submit the other forms (usually IRS 1040 and W2 forms), ask questions about anything that isn't clear, write a letter explaining any unusual circumstances, and do it all *on time*.

Parent's Financial Obligation

I apologize if I am beginning to sound like the voice of doom and gloom. Most families who receive aid are thrilled with the opportunity to provide their child with an excellent education. Despite the financial sacrifices, they would quickly make the same decision all over again. But you should examine your feelings closely before committing to the independent school experience. Try to consider the trade-offs as pragmatically and objectively as possible. Remember that schools rarely can fully meet your financial need, and that what a school expects you to pay may increase over time as tuition rises. Even if the form that comes back to you from ETS says that you qualify for $7,000 in aid, that does not mean the school can afford to grant you that sum.

Although many schools follow the SSS recommendation to the dollar, others use it only as a point of reference and feel comfortable offering a somewhat larger or smaller grant, depending on the family's unique circumstances, the local economy, and the additional expenses beyond tuition at that particular school. Perhaps believing that a child and his family will be more invested in becoming a part of the community if they are making some financial contribution toward the tuition, many schools will not give any grants that cover all of the expenses involved in attending the school. These schools expect every family to make at least a minimal contribution.

Different schools have different policies about divorced or separated parents, but many take the position that both parents have an obligation to contribute to the education of their children, whether they are bound by a legal agreement to do so or not. Although many divorce settlements spell out exactly how much each parent must contribute, some schools may still decide that both parents should be contributing as much as the SSS or school calculations show they can afford. In some instances, a school may ask a parent to contribute less than the court's determination, while in other cases it may be more than the amount stipulated by the divorce settlement.

Many schools will consider the financial resources of both natural parents, if they are living, before they determine how much money to award a student. Therefore, both natural parents will have to provide financial information. If a natural parent has remarried, most schools will also take into consideration his financial obligations to his new family. They will also want financial information about a stepparent who might also have obligations to his natural children. The custodial parent and her spouse are often expected to complete the PFS while the noncustodial parent and his spouse are often asked to submit another financial statement. Each school is trying to get as much relevant, objective data as it can to fairly determine how much money a family can afford to contribute to the cost of sending their child to that school.

FINANCIAL AID AFTER THE FIRST YEAR

Most schools feel an obligation to meet the financial aid needs of its currently enrolled students before they award any money to new students. Unless your family's financial situation changes dramatically, you can assume that the school will continue to give your child a comparable grant every year, but you will still be asked to submit a new PFS and tax forms each year. Some schools expect the family and the school to share the annual tuition increases. In other words, if the tuition goes up $1,000 in one year, most of the financial aid grants would increase to cover part of that $1,000, assuming that the parents' contribution will also need to increase.

Families who are delinquent in paying their school bills may face an uphill battle in their request for aid the following year. If payments become difficult, be sure to talk with your school's business office about a revised payment schedule. Don't just ignore the problem and hope it will go away. Some families, probably in their eagerness and enthusiasm to enroll their child, are overly optimistic and end up committing to payments that are unrealistic. Most schools will try to work with you through these financial issues, but hardly any will be sympathetic to efforts to "stonewall" them or to ignore the bills.

Although some schools outline specific academic requirements for students to continue receiving aid, most anticipate continuing to provide financial aid to students

Unless your financial situation changes, you can assume that the school will continue to give your child a comparable grant every year.

year after year unless those students get in serious disciplinary or academic trouble. On the other hand, don't enroll your child with a small financial aid grant, assuming that the school will give you more money the following year once it realizes how spectacular your child is. Given the steadily increasing interest in private schools, there will be a comparable increase in financial aid applications. Most schools will have modestly increased resources to spread over widely increased requests. Some families naively assume or hope that although they don't qualify for aid this year, that next year, once their child is in the school, the school will look more favorably on their application and grant them aid. Most schools will alter their original judgment only if the family's financial situation changes. In an effort to discourage families from overcommitting to a financial burden, some schools require a family who was denied aid but whose child was admitted to wait two years before they can reapply for financial aid.

Loans

Many schools offer low-interest loan programs that are designed to help parents whose needs the school cannot meet entirely or in part by direct financial aid grants. Other schools that do not offer loan packages are happy to provide information about outside agencies that offer debt financing to families who enroll their children in private schools. Schools are usually resistant about endorsing any particular loan program but can tell you which ones their families are currently using. A typical loan is structured for one to four years of school expenses, with a family's eligibility based on their credit rating. There is usually no prepayment penalty, and you are expected to begin repayment immediately, paying in installments and completing it in eight years. A family is often given the option of rolling the loans into their college loans, and interest is charged quarterly on the amount you pay the school. Be sure to talk with someone at each school to find out about their specific plans.

Many private school families take advantage of various outside agencies that offer interest-free plans that allow a family to pay their bills by making eight payments through the year, beginning in June. Again, each school will provide you with information about any of their payment options.

Merit Scholarships

Some schools award their aid on the basis of documented need but also have money set aside for specific merit scholarships. These financial aid grants go to talented students—be that in athletics, music, or academics—whether their parents can afford the tuition or not. Schools that award scholarships to outstanding students may have a special test or application for those specific scholarships. Each school's admissions office will have materials that describe what type of aid they give and how to apply for these grants.

As you might guess, most of these programs are quite competitive because almost any family would love to have their child receive a merit-based scholarship to a great secondary school. Some schools have established these merit scholarships specifically to attract highly qualified candidates who, without this kind of financial inducement, might overlook a school in their search for the most competitive schools.

Their experience has been that the chance of winning a merit scholarship has enticed many middle-class families

> Although many schools only award need-based aid, you should ask each school whether they offer any merit scholarships that don't take into account financial need. These scholarships attract many strong applicants.

who wouldn't be eligible for financial aid into applying to their school. If their child wins a merit scholarship, the family might choose to send their child even if it means turning down acceptances to more competitive schools that didn't offer any financial inducement.

Many schools offer these merit scholarships in an effort to attract a specific group of students to their school. In some cases, they are attempting to attract athletes; others are looking for racial and ethnic diversity; and others may find these merit-based scholarships a way to compete for academically talented students in an area where there are several very strong independent schools.

Although each school has a finite number of merit scholarships, it is certainly worth the time to investigate the possibilities. As my grandmother used to say, "Nothing ventured, nothing gained." Research and consider schools that offer these scholarships with the same care with which you are investigating all schools. Your quest is to find a good fit for this particular child. Just because your child receives a considerable merit scholarship does not necessarily mean that a particular school is the best place for her to go.

In some instances, the merit scholarship winners may find themselves in an environment where, for the very reasons they won the scholarship, they stick out and feel like an anomaly. Although certainly some very talented children would enjoy and thrive in a setting where they were clearly "the best" student, athlete, or musician, many other adolescents would be uncomfortable.

Given many childrens' preoccupation with their peers and fitting in, it is not surprising that many kids, including some of the brightest and most talented, would prefer to be in a place where there are other equally shining lights. Other talented adolescents need the motivation that can come from competing with other equally talented peers.

Again, this is all about fit, and finding the best fit requires some real thought about your child and what makes him tick. If you're struggling with this issue, it might be helpful to ask some adults who know your child well, especially his teachers, who will have a sense of how he responds to competition and what seems to motivate him to do his best.

All that said, it is certainly worth investigating whether there are any merit scholarships available at schools that might provide a good fit for your child. As with applying for financial aid, you have nothing to lose but the time it takes to fill out the forms.

PAYING FOR COLLEGE

Families who are worried about how they will pay for a private school are often haunted by tales of staggering college tuitions that still await them. No sooner will they finish with the private school bills than they will be faced with even larger numbers.

These are real concerns—college expenses are high. Many families pay well over $30,000 a year for tuition, room, and board. The good news is that there are enormous opportunities for financial aid, scholarships, loans, and work-study programs. State schools are much less expensive than private colleges, and families who are willing to do the necessary research can find many excellent, affordable college opportunities for their children.

More and more families feel that the education their children receive in the elementary and secondary levels is so critical that they are willing to make significant financial sacrifices to ensure that their children go to good schools.

Few college admissions officers or professors would argue that a child's character is formed in college. Most readily acknowledge that character formation takes place long before a child steps on to a college campus. Most professors also quickly acknowledge than many critical life skills, including students' attitudes toward learning, are formed earlier than their freshman year of college.

This kind of thinking has led many parents to do whatever is possible—including relocating, commuting long distances, and making considerable financial sacrifices—to send their children to the best secondary schools. One could also argue that with the best preparation, most children will have a substantially better chance of being accepted to a wide range of strong colleges where there will be numerous financial aid and scholarship possibilities.

It is difficult to predict how your child will do in school and what opportunities will come her way. It is also important to find a balance between wanting your child to work hard, do well, and be appreciative of her opportunities while at the same time not overwhelming her with pressure to perform at an unrealistic level. In a best-case scenario, you might have to sacrifice a bit in order to send your child to a private school. It's a great fit, she does well, and she is able to attend a great college at a manageable

Many families feel that the education their children receive in elementary and secondary school is so critical that they will make significant financial sacrifices to send their children to good schools.

cost to you and your family. You also need to be ready to accept a less-than-perfect scenario in which you sacrifice to send your child to a private school, and she does okay but not brilliantly. She goes on to an average college and you are left wondering whether you made the right choice.

Remember, your tuition dollars are not just about buying a ticket to a college. When you choose to send your child to a private school, you're hoping to give her a better chance to learn, to find her strengths, and to compensate for her weaknesses. You are looking for a good fit, a sense of community, and a safe environment.

But at the end of the day, given that you can't guarantee the final results, you'll need to decide whether or not having your child attend a private school is worth the financial sacrifices.

Choosing Where To Go

By the time March finally arrives, you and your child will probably be incredibly nervous and a bit tired of worrying about the whole search process. You've talked about and listened to more information about private schools than you ever wanted to know. But if all went according to plan (and as adults, we know that rarely happens), on or about March 14, you and your child will be faced with choosing among several acceptances from the schools where she most wanted to go. It doesn't matter whether these turn out to be the schools you initially thought were her reaches, targets, or safeties. As you learn more and more about the various schools, one that you originally thought of as a safety could become more appealing. Sometimes a reach starts to feel out of a child's league, perhaps too big and too competitive. It's amazing how, as you accumulate more information and gain a better sense of your child and of the ethos and character of each school, you become much more versed on what the options are and how your child might respond in each of them. While many people begin the process with some preconceived notions or an idealized view of one or two fairly well-known schools, by the end of an extensive search, parents and children often come to realize that there are probably several schools where they could be happy and feel they fit in.

REJECTIONS

In today's competitive market, you need to be prepared to help your child—and yourself—deal with some rejections. For many children, this will be their first experience with being judged and found, for whatever reason, lacking. The truth is, your child may be imminently qualified for the school, but it simply didn't have room to take all of its qualified applicants.

That is not how it's going to feel to most kids who get turned down. They will feel like they failed, like they didn't make the grade. Even though you will be disappointed, too, be careful to share your feelings only with your spouse or close friend when you are out of your child's earshot. Be careful, because she will probably be watching you like a hawk, ready to pounce on anything that even hints of your disappointment with her. At some level, despite your very best intentions, she will probably feel, at least briefly, that she has failed you. This will pass.

Sometimes the school's letter will include the number of applicants they have had for the few seats they could fill. Be sure to point this out to your child, who probably rushed right past that part of the letter. Most private schools are experiencing a dramatic increase in applications, so many qualified kids are being wait listed or turned down. You need to remind your child that this is about numbers, not about his talents, performance, or worth as a human. Too many children read far too much into their rejection letter, as though they have been turned down not by a school but by life.

> **Most private schools are experiencing a dramatic increase in applications, and many terrific kids are being wait listed or turned down.**

If, on the other hand, your child had not been working hard and his grades were poor or had fallen, it's probably appropriate to point out, calmly and quietly, that admission to the school was competitive and it probably accepted kids with strong academic records.

If, with all the objectivity you can muster, you really do not understand why your child was turned down by a school, give the admissions office a call. I suggest this not because I think you will be able to change the verdict but rather because there might be some serious differences between the way you see your child and the way the school saw her. Calmly ask them if they could explain the reasoning that led to your child's rejection. Listen carefully, even if you don't like or agree with what you are hearing. It's important to learn how the school saw your child. This insight could be helpful when she applies for a summer job or even to another school or to college.

The possibility of dealing with at least one rejection should serve as a good reminder throughout your search to be mindful of what you say about the public school options. It's important to realize that, especially if your child only applies to a few schools, she may end up staying in the public school system. It is going to be a lot easier for her and you to make that transition and move beyond her initial disappointment if both of you haven't spent a lot of time bashing the school system.

WAIT LISTING

It is not a good use of your time or the school's to appeal to them to reconsider a rejection. Schools create wait lists so they will always have other acceptable applicants waiting in the wings, should they need them. Given the number of applicants, your child's stack of letters might also include a wait list. If so, it would be appropriate to call the admission officer and try to get some sense of the chances that your child will be taken off the wait list and accepted. Most schools establish a wait list of students who they think would do well at the school and to whom they plan to offer admission if there are any more available spots. In a sense, the wait list is the school's insurance that they will have a full school come September. Many families have to withdraw their children from school because of job relocation. Private schools have learned to cope with this by keeping a wait list of families who are eager to join the school at any point in the year that an opening becomes available.

Each school deals with wait lists in its own way, and some schools vary their use from year to year. Many schools accept more kids than they have room for right from the start in the assumption that some of the kids they accept will decide not to come. In a given year when their yield (number of accepted kids who choose to accept the offer) is high, they might not need to go to their wait list at all.

Another school—and certainly this could include a school that routinely shares applicants with a small group of comparable schools—expects to go to its wait list every year. That school consistently accepts a group of exceptional students who view the school as a safety and therefore go to one of their stronger rivals if accepted. The school protects itself by wait listing a lot of strong candidates, expecting to go back to many of them with a later acceptance.

You should call each school where your child has been wait listed to get some specific answers about the numbers. Many schools will tell you exactly how many children they wait listed, but they won't tell you where your child is on the list. Other schools will readily tell you what number your child is on the list and whether they anticipate going to the wait list at all. Although this lack of clarity can be frustrating, don't push and run the risk of alienating the admissions staff.

Try to see the situation from the school's perspective. It is trying to be helpful to you, but it is also trying to keep its options open. The school doesn't know yet which or how many students to whom it offered admissions will be coming, and it does not yet know whether it will need more boys or girls, more musicians or athletes.

You and your child need to decide where this wait-list school belongs on her list of choices. If she has already been accepted to a school she would prefer to attend, then call this school right away and ask them to remove your child's name from the list. It is important to do this in a timely fashion so you don't interfere with another wait-listed child's chance to go there.

> Before you make a final, nonrefundable commitment to a school, be sure to remove your child's name from any wait lists she may be on.

If the wait-list school is your child's first choice, call to tell them that this is your child's first choice, and ask to remain on the wait list. Some families remain on the wait list until the fall, and occasionally a place opens up just as school begins. Children who had returned to the public schools and, therefore, had not signed a contract with another private school, often leap on these last minute opportunities, even if it means they will have missed preseason soccer practice or the first few days of class.

Other wait-listed families have spent a great deal of emotional energy adjusting to the fact that they won't be going to the school that wait listed them. For them, this last minute or even midsummer acceptance doesn't seem worth yet another emotional upheaval. Schools realize this and try to go to their wait-listed students in a timely manner. Families occasionally get relocated or decide that they cannot cope with the financial obligations and turn down their acceptances right before the summer deadline for the first semester's tuition. In general, most of the wait-listed movement happens by July 1. Again, should you find yourself in a wait-list position, talk with the admissions office about their past experience and policies.

If you and your child are remaining on a wait list with the hope of being accepted, you need to give some thought as to how to interact with the admissions office. I think it's appropriate for your child to write a letter, probably no more than a page, telling the school that she wants to stay on their wait list and reiterating why she wants to go there. Although you certainly don't want to bombard them with more information or be seen as a pest, if your child receives any recognition while you're waiting, be sure to pass it on to the school. Should she receive an award at the end of the year, be a member of a championship team, or be accepted for a particularly interesting or unusual summer course or job, drop the school a brief note. But be careful—you don't want to inundate the school with so many letters that the school has to create one of those dreaded "fat" folders.

FINANCIAL CONSIDERATIONS

The financial aspects of the acceptances your child receives may help determine your final choice. Although schools use a common form to determine your financial need, each school's individual analysis can lead to quite different offers. A school with a lot of financial aid to give will frequently end up offering your family a substantially larger grant than another school that really wants your child just as badly but has more limited financial resources.

For some families—especially those with more than one child hoping to attend private school—the finances determine the decision. They must choose the school that will cost them the least. If this is your situation, it's critical that you get an accurate picture of what the costs will be. The bad news is that in most private schools there are predictable costs that could go way beyond the tuition. The admissions office can give you information about these costs, which might include books, field trips, lunch, transportation, and athletic uniforms and equipment. Some schools publish a range of these costs per grade. Although they won't be able to tell you down to the last dollar, they should certainly be prepared to give you some guidance. Don't be embarrassed to ask; they get asked this constantly. The only people who end up being embarrassed are the parents who do not ask and are in for a sometimes unpleasant wake-up call.

Many families decide to choose the more expensive private school if they think going there will help their child secure scholarships and grants when she gets to college. Many colleges and universities can put together generous financial packages that include grants, loans, and work-study options. Knowing that, many families decide it is worth the financial tightening for four years to put their child in an excellent school that may help her get into a great college.

A few parents have had some success in appealing their initial offer of financial aid. In most cases, this involves a lengthy conversation with the financial aid officer and being able to convince him that the school has, for some reason, not understood your financial situation. Although some schools may be willing to recalculate your aid, others are not or don't have any more money to offer. This conversation occasionally leads to a reassessment, and the school is able to offer you a larger grant. Consider yourself fortunate if that happens to you. Again, remember that badgering the financial aid officer or making a pest of yourself can be counterproductive.

Even after a school makes an increased financial aid offer, you still may feel that you and your family simply cannot come up with the amount of money the school is expecting from you. Many families, even when both the parents and child love the same school, decide that the required financial sacrifices would not be worth it. Although they are confident that their child would thrive in the school and get a great education, they cannot face three or four years with limited vacations, little money for any kind of entertainment, and the dread that can come from feeling like you're always behind in your payments. Parents rightfully worry that their child will feel tremendous pressure to perform and will eventually resent the decision to switch schools. Other families facing the exact same circumstances and worries conclude that it's worth it. There is neither a right answer nor an easy decision.

CHOOSING

If you and your child find yourself looking at several acceptances, and finances are not a major issue, you still have to find some way to choose. I am assuming that you allowed your child to apply only to schools that were acceptable to both of you. This can be a much more difficult phase of the process if you are in a situation where your child is eager to go to a school that you never liked from the beginning. If you've landed there—and it can happen to the most well-meaning parents—you need to weigh your hesitation about the school against your child's enthusiasm for it. Be open about sharing your concerns, but avoid a scenario in which you list five million defects but still allow your child to attend. Your critique will not be forgotten easily and may come back to haunt you.

Second Visits

Families will frequently decide to go back and revisit the schools that have offered their child admission. Almost all schools welcome second visits, and many schedule formal visiting days for their accepted students. Some host early evening gatherings so parents and students have an opportunity to speak with teachers, administrators, current parents, and other students. Remembering our earlier discussion in Chapter 4 might help your child focus her attention on specific features of each school. Again, written notes and checklists can make a tremendous difference. You may also find this second visit a great opportunity to share your concerns or questions with the admissions officer, who may be able to alleviate your worries. Feel free to ask for the names of current parents with whom you could speak. It's especially helpful if the school can give you the names of current parents whose children either came from your child's old school or who have interests or abilities that are similar to your child's.

Once their acceptance letters are mailed, more and more schools have begun launching what can best be described as campaigns to convince the kids they accepted to choose their school. Copying what used to be done only at the college level, coaches and sometimes teachers, parents, or students will call your son urging him to come and offering to answer any questions. Although these conversations can seem awkward, especially if your child is fairly shy or quiet, they can give you some useful information and give you a better sense of the people in each community.

Not all schools get into this kind of courting, so if you don't receive any phone calls or additional letters, do not misread this as a lack of interest on the school's part. They want your child to attend, or else they wouldn't have accepted him. The truth is, if you and your child have been thoughtful and careful in determining where to apply, he will probably be fine at any of the schools you are now reexamining. But if you still have questions or concerns, make the most of this courting time to get them answered. Ask if you can sit in on one or two classes or talk with a few teachers. Although many schools cannot schedule this for every family that visits, they are often willing to work something out for their accepted students.

Reexamining Schools

If you have a particularly able child, look for evidence that she will be challenged and stretched. Again, ask for the names of parents or talk with the department head or senior faculty member in the area where your child either excels or is particularly interested. If your child will need some support, be sure to see if the school has a resource teacher or if they expect you to find and pay for an outside tutor. If your child is hoping to take Advanced Placement (AP) courses, find out if they sign up for those classes by student choice or teacher recommendation. Are the electives he is most interested in offered every year, on a rotating schedule, or only when there is sufficient enrollment? Be sure to get these important questions answered before you make a decision. You don't want to feel dissatisfied or resentful later because you made certain assumptions that turned out to be incorrect. Many of these curricular matters are not clear in the standard admissions materials. Too often, children and their parents think they understand the course options but are disappointed and frustrated when they don't turn out as they expected.

Now that you and your child have a choice, be sure that you really want to leave your current school. It's interesting that some students, and even some parents, at first think they want to go to another school, but in the end they decide to stay where they are. In the best of all worlds, you will be comfortable letting your child make this final choice. You want him to be excited and enthusiastic about going to the school in the fall. That said, some parents feel so strongly about the need to find a better school for their child that they move to a private school despite strong resistance from their child.

In many ways this resistance is understandable and predictable. Change is scary, and leaving your friends can be terrifying. Even a child who was initially enthusiastic about the search may get a case of cold feet once the desired acceptance is in hand. Be prepared ahead of time for this possibility. If you feel this is the right thing to do and will be a good fit for your child, you may be forced to make the decision for him. You have a more informed perspective of the advantages and disadvantages that a change may bring.

Now that you and your child have a choice, be sure that you really want to leave your current school.

One final (and perhaps unnecessary) caveat before you choose a school: If you have any serious misgivings or real discomfort with an important feature of the school, don't go there thinking you will change it. Most private schools are willing to consider innovations, but by and large, you're not likely to make fundamental changes to their sense of mission or philosophy. If you're hoping to convince a school to change its uniform policy or the role of religion in the community or to de-emphasize athletics, don't go there. Although you might have some success in having them reconsider the question, there is a good chance that both you and the school will feel that you and your child could have found a better fit elsewhere.

As a private school parent, there will certainly be times when you question or disagree with a decision the school made—but you don't want to enter into that relationship knowing that you disagree on fundamental issues. Private schools are not places of rapid change; many of them have scores of satisfied and grateful alumni and parents who are convinced that the school has done a great job and should continue to do things much the same way it has for decades.

WHEN YOU HAVE TWO APPLICANTS

Some families find themselves in the unusual and potentially difficult situation of having two children apply to the same school. Different parents seem equally emphatic about the virtues of separating or keeping twins or siblings together. I don't think there is a right answer. It depends on the children—how much distance, both physically and emotionally, they want and need. Some twins go through twelve years of school together, blissfully happy and at a real loss when not together. Other siblings, not just twins, need to have their own places, their own schools. One might live in the shadow of the other, which is difficult for both.

A family that has two or more children applying at the same time to the same school walks on complicated ground. In the best-case scenario, it's easy. Both kids are wildly enthusiastic about the school, both of them and their parents are comfortable with having them attend the same school, and they have both been accepted. Change the outcome, though, and you have a knotty problem.

One of your children gets accepted by Wonderful Academy and the other one gets turned down or wait listed. It is interesting to note that some schools will do almost anything to avoid this dilemma. Some schools will not accept the stronger and perfectly acceptable twin if they feel they cannot accept the other one.

Needless to say, no two families are alike and neither are the relationships between any two siblings in the same family. I have seen many families turn down an acceptance for one child if their other child was rejected. Other families are comfortable separating their children and sending them to two different schools, even though they had hoped to send them together. You need to consider not only the damage to the self-confidence and ego of your child who was turned down but also the academic and developmental needs of your child who was accepted. This is not easy parenting.

Families facing an acceptance and a wait list are usually more comfortable accepting the one spot while holding on to the wait list, hoping another spot will open up in the late spring or early summer. Under these particularly difficult circumstances, most admissions officers will make a real effort to share with you a realistic picture of their anticipated use of the wait list and your child's place on that list.

FINAL STEPS

Once you and your family have made your decision, it is courteous to let each school know what it is. Your response to each school allows them to contact families on their wait list in a timely manner, which in turn lets those families finalize their plans. If you are looking at several acceptances or wait lists and can eliminate any of them—perhaps even before you make a final decision—do it as soon as you are sure. Your release of a spot may be critical in the decision-making process of another family.

The Transition to a Private School

You've finally made your decision and sent off the first check to your child's new private school. But just as you breathe that sigh of relief, you find your mailbox flooded with brochures, forms, and applications to be filled out before your child sets off for her first day at her new school. Although the packet for each school will vary, there are some standard items that need your careful and prompt attention. Although schools try to be flexible—especially with new students and parents—they really need your help to meet the various deadlines for course registration, placement tests, and medical information.

PLACEMENT TESTS

Many schools ask their new students to come in during the spring to take placement tests, perhaps in math and in a foreign language. These are used to determine an appropriate math course and to see if your child belongs in level 1,2, or 3 of the foreign language that she will be studying. Students who are beginning a new language or who have never studied a foreign language will not be asked to take the language assessment. Although your child wants to do his best on these tests, they should not be a cause for worry or stress. His acceptance will not be rescinded on the basis of these tests.

Chapter 9

Following or at the same time as these placements tests, your child will be asked for input on his schedule. Many ninth and tenth graders have a prescribed program with a choice of a foreign language and perhaps one other elective or a choice between two history courses. Most schools allow their juniors and seniors more options in their course selections. Your child may have an opportunity to discuss his course choices with his adviser, class dean, or scheduling officer. This is a good opportunity to look at different four-year plans that focus on different student interests. Although it is appropriate for your child to take the lead in these conversations and in choosing his electives, you can and should get involved. Many high school students can get caught up in choosing to take or avoid taking a course without really considering the long-term repercussions of that choice. You want to avoid having your child make any selections without knowing if they preclude any later options.

SUMMER MAILINGS

Over the summer, you and your child will receive what seems like an endless stream of mail from her new school. Schools work hard to bundle this mail in one or two large mailings in which you will receive information about transportation options, the year's calendar, summer reading expectations, preseason practices and try-outs, uniform orders, health forms, and invitations to new student and parent activities. These mailings can be overwhelming at times and are best managed if they are always kept in the same place and are sorted through immediately.

1. **School calendar:** Put the year's calendar in a conspicuous place and take note of any back-to-school evenings and parent–teacher conferences. You need to make every conceivable effort to attend these events, even if it requires elaborate babysitting arrangements for your other children or taking time off from work. Your child's teachers expect you to be there—it's the best way to learn about your child's experience.

2. **Medical forms:** Make any necessary medical appointments immediately. Most schools require an annual physical and expect to receive the completed health forms before school opens. Unfortunately, many families wait until the last moment to schedule these appointments and find that their pediatrician can't fit them in. Most schools require specific health forms for athletes who expect to participate in a preseason. Many of the preseasons begin in early August, so those doctor appointments become more scarce.

3. **Transportation:** If you are unsure about your best transportation option, call the admissions office, which can give you more information and probably the names and numbers of any other school families who live near you. Although some parents enjoy driving their kids to and from school every day, because it gives them a better chance of hearing more about school, there are advantages to carpooling. Car pools, vans, and buses, which will no doubt initially seem lonely and challenging to a new student, may eventually lead to some wonderful friendships. Be sure to explore any afterschool

athletic or artistic obligations that might make it difficult or even unadvisable for you to try to set up an afternoon car pool. Many private school students stay at school until 6 p.m. on a regular basis. Some schools offer a late bus to allow more kids to participate in afterschool programs. There is no question that playing on a team or joining a club is an important way for students to feel connected to a new community. Even though this might present transportation challenges, try to find a way to make it possible for your child to participate in activities that interest her.

4. **Summer reading:** Needless to say, be sure your child has time to complete any required summer reading in a timely manner. Although some eager new students rush out and do all their assigned reading in early June, they might forget information from the books by September. This will depend on the amount of required reading and how your child is spending his summer. Some private schools may not spend much time or may not quiz their students on the summer reading; other schools may focus on summer reading assignments for the whole month of September. Your child doesn't want to run the risk of being unprepared. He needs to have done all the required reading. Some schools provide copies of the assigned summer reading books, which certainly makes it easy for the students and their parents. If this is not the case, you might want to buy or borrow them right after you get the list. Several area schools may require some of the same books, which can lead to lengthy back orders.

GETTING TO KNOW PEOPLE

Over the summer and early in the fall, many schools schedule informal parties for new students, and some welcome new parents to special gatherings at both the school and at the homes of current parents. Although some kids and parents are nervous about these encounters, convince your child that these are great opportunities to meet people in her new community. Private schools are eager to welcome new parents as well as their children. Most send out volunteer forms over the summer, hoping to entice parents to help with projects during the year. Even if both you and your spouse work full-time, it would be important to find some activity for which you could volunteer. Working on a school auction, selling refreshments during the play's intermission, or helping stuff a mailing are all good ways to meet other parents and feel like you are contributing to the school. Since private schools now include many more families in which both parents work full-time, they are having trouble recruiting volunteers. The parents who do find a way to get involved in at least one activity tend to feel more connected to their child's school.

Parenting adolescents is difficult enough in a small confined neighborhood; it is noticeably harder if you don't know your child's friends or their parents. Many private day schools attract students from an hour in every direction, and therefore the school itself becomes the most likely place for parents to meet. Recognizing how important this parent networking is, many schools host informal gatherings each fall for the parents in each grade. Make the most of these early opportunities and at later events during the year by seeking out and introducing yourself to the parents of any of your child's new friends. There is no question that it's easier to stay on top of the normal drug, alcohol, or party issues if you feel like you can pick up the phone and compare notes with another parent.

TUITION INSURANCE

Somewhere in your pile of school mail you may notice a reference to tuition insurance. This fairly inexpensive insurance can be critical for a family who might be relocated midyear. Some families who are new to independent schools may not realize that they have signed a contract to pay the year's tuition whether their child finishes the year or not. If you move or, heaven forbid, your child is miserably unhappy or gets expelled, you are still liable for the year's tuition. Tuition insurance will protect you from losing your money in that situation. Most families never purchase it and never need it, but if you feel, for whatever reason, that it might be necessary, be sure to find out what the school offers.

PARENTS AS PARTNERS TO THE SCHOOL

At the opening meetings—either those specifically for new parents or larger ones for all parents—you will no doubt hear numerous references to the school's desire to establish an open, honest partnership with you, the parents. Do your part right from the start to make this happen. It's important to figure out the appropriate line of communication and not take your concerns too far up the "food chain." Most schools publish a handbook that includes an incredible amount of information, including the school's preferred protocol for dealing with problems. Many schools will encourage you to call the specific teacher if there is an academic issue. If that seems awkward, call your child's adviser or homeroom teacher. Find out early who the appropriate person is and then make an effort to reach out to him. He will be eager to get to know your child as well as you.

I'm not suggesting that you pour out your child's life history and every family issue that you can remember, but you should certainly share any major concerns that you have about your child or an issue in your family that might impact your child. The adviser doesn't need to know all the details, but he should know if you and your spouse have recently separated or if one of your parents is gravely ill. He will be interested in hearing how you think your child is adjusting to his new school, and you may also learn a lot from him about how your child feels and acts at school. Sometimes these pictures are very different. Some children seem fine at home, profess to like the new school, and yet seem lonely and unhappy while at school. For others, the reverse is true. Sharing your observations with each other may give you both a more accurate read of your child's adjustment.

Most schools publish a handbook that includes information on the school's preferred protocol for dealing with problems.

As you get to know your child's adviser, homeroom teacher, or class dean, remember that just like you, he will appreciate hearing good news as well as bad. As parents, we often wish our child's teacher would occasionally call with a compliment rather than when there is something worrisome to report. An occasional call just to thank or compliment the adviser could also help to strengthen your relationship.

Annual Giving

As remarkable as it may seem, considering that private school families pay tuitions as high as $25,000 a year, almost all schools ask their families to donate money annually. A student's tuition does not cover the school's cost to educate that student. The gap is made up in large part by gifts to the school from its graduates and past and present parents. When schools approach foundations and corporations for gifts, one of the first things they're asked is what percentage of their parents support the annual fund. Although some parents are capable of giving large sums, schools are eager to have a large percentage of their parents participate and give something, no matter how small the amount.

HOMEWORK AND HOME

Prior to beginning private school, your child may have done quite well in school without spending a lot of time on his homework. If so, private school life will change that dramatically and probably immediately. Most private school teachers assign considerable homework from the first day of school on, with little relief. They are eager to teach, ambitious about what they want their course to include, and expect to have students who are willing and used to working hard.

Many private school students spend most of every school evening and much of most weekends doing homework. For kids who play on athletic teams, sing in the chorus, write for the school newspaper, or spend considerable time participating in extracurricular activities, managing homework

is difficult. These other activities are time-consuming but
also an important and exciting part of the high school
experience. Although you might have to insist that your
child limit the number of these activities, it's important to
realize how significant they can be.

It is appropriate for high school students to assume
responsibility for their homework. Unless they or their
teacher requests that you hear or proofread some piece of
work, don't get into the habit of checking their assignments.
On the other hand, it is absolutely appropriate for you to
do everything you can to create an environment that is
conducive to studying. Turning off the television, limiting
phone calls, and establishing a quiet place to work will
help. Sadly, but not surprisingly, many parents have found
it advisable to monitor the use of a computer to make sure
kids do not spend hours surfing the net or hanging out in
chat rooms instead of researching a term paper. Despite the
advice we were given years ago about creating a quiet,
private study place away from the rest of the family, many
parents have been happier having the computer in a space
that is more central and easier to monitor.

GRADES AND COMMENTS

Your child's grades and teacher comments, which are usually personalized and extensive, will quickly give you some
sense of whether your child is preparing his homework
appropriately. Some students, especially those for whom
their old school was not very challenging, may have a

traumatic transition to the workload and academic expectations of a private school. Don't be alarmed if he does not immediately achieve at the level he was used to in his former school.

If his first grades seem alarming rather than just a little lower than what he was receiving in past years, or if your child seems discouraged, contact the appropriate teacher(s) or his adviser. Do not jump to this conclusion after one poor paper. Many teachers traditionally grade their first assignments with sharp pencils. Their experience has been that this is an effective way to jolt their students into a sharper focus and increased effort. After the first couple of weeks, you and your child will have a better sense of whether or not he needs additional help. Most private school teachers are willing to spend time outside of class working with individual students. If your child is having difficulty, strongly encourage her to seek out the teacher and ask for help. If the extra sessions do not seem to provide sufficient support, explore the possibility of a tutor. It is important to put the necessary support in place so your child does not become discouraged by the transition to private school.

> **Many teachers grade their first assignments with sharp pencils. Their experience has been that this is an effective way to jolt students into a sharper focus and increased effort.**

NEW AND OLD FRIENDS

If your child is still seeing his friends from his former school, be prepared for their commentary on his new, studious, and boring life. With considerably less free time, it will be increasingly difficult for him to hang out with his old friends, who may not be facing comparable academic

demands. This can seem even worse if he is—which is
certainly to be expected—still not sure whether he is going
to make any friends in his new school. He's being asked to
give up his old friends before he is confident that he will
ever find any substitutes.

Reassure him by reminding him of why you and he
both wanted him to go to this school. Assure him that it
always takes time to make new friends. Encourage him to
pursue at least one school activity—a sport, club, or community service project. Many shy adolescents need to be
encouraged to call a classmate for an assignment or clarifica-
tion of something that went on in class. Similarly, some
kids who are prone to come on too strong might need a
gentle reminder that they neither need to nor are they
expected to find a new best friend by the end of Day 2.

BUMPS ALONG THE WAY

Although for some kids the transition to a new school is
seamless and everything they and you ever hoped it could
be, for others the first few weeks can be a challenge. They
might have spent so much time fantasizing about how
wonderful their new school would be that it can never
measure up to those expectations.

Occasionally, there are snafus that in the long run will
seem minor but at the moment seem monumental. Students
sometimes end up in the wrong section; your gifted soccer
player might get cut from the varsity team and the luck of
the draw might make it hard for her to find friends quickly.

School Clothing

Over the years I have encountered more than one unhappy parent who was facing a pile of newly purchased clothes that were being rejected by a new student who was eager to do everything she could to fit in with her new friends. Each school has a slightly different culture, with its own fashions and tastes. It might be wise and save a lot of money and possibly some tears, not to buy many new school clothes or even a backpack until school opens. Of course, some kids are oblivious to this type of peer pressure, but others would be happier blending into the crowd. It may take your son or daughter a few weeks to sort that out. Be patient—try to remember how you felt at that age.

BOARDING SCHOOL

There is no question that having your child go off to boarding school for the first time is a major change for both you and your child. Although a few families find great relief in no longer engaging in daily arguments about clothes, homework, and curfews, for many other children and their parents this separation is both shocking and lonely. As parents, most of us have been conditioned to expect this "empty nest" syndrome when our kids go off to college. For boarding school parents and students, it comes three or four years earlier and can be more jarring.

Every family will react differently. In families where there are still several siblings at home or where this child is merely following in the footsteps of her older siblings who went away to school, the departure can be less traumatic. Having your first or only child go away to school at age 14 can be a huge change in your life. Although many kids are homesick initially, most of them (and most of their parents) adapt and adjust nicely to this change.

Helping your child navigate through the first few weeks at boarding school can be stressful. You know your child well and are the best judge of how to support her. New boarders often need to be reminded that most people feel homesick and nervous in a new situation. They need to know that you love and miss them, but spare them the details of your temporary misery. The thought of you sitting home crying will not speed up their adjustment.

With e-mail and cell phones, some parents are in almost hourly contact with their children. For families that operated like that before a child went off to boarding school, constant communication might seem natural and helpful. But many kids need some time by themselves to meet other kids and to start feeling like they're making themselves a new home away from home.

When you do talk, try to be upbeat and confident so your child will feel better soon. This is a time when kids are scrutinizing your words, expression, and tone for any hint that you think this was a bad decision. No matter how much you miss her, don't focus on that. You do not need to add to your child's misery and worries by detailing your own sense of loss and loneliness. Work hard to give her the impression that you are going about your normal life. Encourage her to join a club or try out for a team or a play. Give her the same advice and encouragement you would be giving her if she had just started at a local day school.

> At some schools, most boarders go home or away every open weekend, leaving the few who stay at campus feeling isolated and lonely. Other schools host weekend activities to integrate new students into the community.

Be sure to attend Parents' Weekend and talk with your child's adviser or dorm parent about how often you should visit and how often your child should come home for weekends. As tempting as it may be to see your child every weekend, it might make it more difficult for him to make that initial adjustment. Seek the advice of someone in the admissions office or other parents. Again, every school has a different culture.

Talking with other seasoned boarding school parents will give you an important perspective. Although each child is different, hearing other tales of homesickness and recovery may make you feel better and provide you with some important tips on how to survive and help your child make the adjustment to this separation.

Although letter writing seems to have fallen out of fashion, many find it soothing and therapeutic to write to their boarding school children on a regular basis. Modest care packages, and particularly those that include favorite treats, are always appreciated by your child and her new friends.

Given the natural reticence of many adolescents to talk about their lives, as boarding school parents, you will have to work hard at finding ways to spend enough time talking or visiting to learn about your child's new life. You will probably be pleasantly surprised to see how independent she has become. Just as in a day school, it's important to share your observations with your child's adviser or teacher; boarding school parents are also eager to hear from dorm parents about their child's transition. In an effort to spare their child any embarrassment or to avoid sending a message that they are worried, many parents make secret calls to the dorm parent, adviser, or teacher. Given the rather typical adolescent resistance to sharing with their parents the details parents most want to hear, it's understandable that many boarding school parents resort to these clandestine phone calls, particularly in the first few weeks of separation.

Expect some tears and some homesickness, but also be assured that most kids, be they in day or boarding school, adjust, make the transition, and are able to make the most of the many opportunities that private schools offer them.

Resources

2000-2001 Educational Register (published annually by Vincent/Curtis, Boston), telephone: 800-354-4081 (toll-free) or 617-536-0100; fax: 617-536-8098; E-mail: register@vincentcurtis.com.

Association of Military Colleges and Schools of the United States, 9429 Garden Court, Potomac, Maryland 20854-3964; telephone: 301-765-0695; fax: 301-983-0583; Web site: www.amcsus.org.

Boarding Schools Directory (available from National Association of Independent Schools, 1620 L Street NW, Washington, D.C. 20036-5605; telephone: 202-973-9700).

Educational Records Bureau, 345 East 47th Street, New York, New York 10017; telephone: 800-989-3721 (toll-free).

Friends Council on Education, 1507 Cherry Street, Philadelphia, Pennsylvania 19102; telephone: 215-241-7245; fax: 215-241-7299; Web site: forum.swarthmore.edu/fce.

International Boys School Coalition, 285 SOM Center Road, Hunting Valley, Ohio 44022; telephone: 216-831-2200.

The Maine Coast Semester/Chewonki Foundation, 485 Chewonki Neck Road, Wiscasset, Maine 04573; telephone: 207-882-7323.

National Association of Episcopal Schools, 815 Second Avenue, Suite 313, New York, New York 10017; telephone: 212-716-6134; fax: 212-286-9366; Web site: www.naes.org.

National Association of Independent Schools, 1620 L Street NW, Washington, D.C. 20036-5605; telephone: 202-973-9700.

The National Coalition of Girls' Schools, 228 Main Street, Concord, Massachusetts 01742; telephone: 978-287-4485; fax: 978-287-6014; Web site: www.ncgs.org.

Network of Sacred Heart Schools, 860 Beacon Street, Newton Centre, Massachusetts 02459-1879; telephone: 617-965-2766; fax: 617-965-6937; Web site: www.sofie.org/network.

Orton Dyslexia Society, 71 West 23rd Street, New York, New York 10011; telephone: 212-691-1930.

Peterson's Private Secondary Schools 1999–2000.

Secondary School Admissions Testing Bureau (SSATB), 12 Stockton Street, Princeton, New Jersey 08540; telephone: 800-442-SSAT (toll-free).

School and Student Service for Financial Aid (SSS), administered by Educational Testing Service, Rosedale Road, Princeton, New Jersey 08541; telephone: 609-921-9000.

Sample Applications

PRELIMINARY APPLICATION: SCHOOL A

This card must be returned with a $35 fee in order to initiate the application process

Name of Student _____
First   Middle   Last

Applicant for grade _____

Birth date ____/____/____ **Male** ☐ **Female** ☐ **Nickname** _____

Address

_____

_____
                              street address

city   state   zip code   country

Telephone: Home ( ) _____ Parent's work: ( ) _____

Present School _____

Address of school _____

_____

Applying for _____ **Boarding or Day** _____
                   Year

Has this child applied to this school before? ☐ Yes ☐ No

If yes, when? _____

Does this child have a sibling applying for admission to this school this year?

☐ Yes ☐ No **Name** _____

Relatives now or previously attending this school:

_____

_____

Name of Mother _____
                First   Middle   Last

Name of Father _____
                First   Middle   Last

Name of parent or guardian with whom this student resides _____

Will this student be a candidate for financial aid? ☐ Yes ☐ No

SAMPLE APPLICATION: SCHOOL B

Application Procedures

Upper School Application Procedures

Entering Grades 9–12

Thank you for your application. Please follow the instructions below to ensure the successful completion of the admission process.

I. APPLICATION

Please return the following:

_____ Completed application with parent signature

_____ Completed student application

_____ Transcript request card with parent signature

_____ Application fee of $50 (please put in writing request for waiver if a financial hardship)

II. CAMPUS VISIT

Upon receipt of the application, the Admissions Office will call to schedule an interview. Students will also be asked to complete a writing sample at this time.

Parents are encouraged to accompany students to this interview, which will include a discussion of curriculum and school programs and a tour of school facilities. The visit will last approximately two hours.

180
Game Plan for Getting into Private School
www.petersons.com

III. TESTING

The SSAT is required of all applicants to grades 6–12. The SSAT Bulletin of Information and registration form are enclosed for your convenience. Please submit the form directly to the SSAT. We strongly urge you to use the November and December test dates. Please note registration deadlines.

IV. TEACHER RECOMMENDATIONS

Please ask two current teachers to complete the appropriate recommendation forms after November 15. The third recommendation should be from a guidance counselor, school principal, or former teacher of the student. Be sure to provide recommendation writers with stamped envelopes addressed to the school.

V. FINANCIAL AID

Please indicate your interest in financial aid on the parent application. In December we will send you the forms necessary for filing with the School and Student Service for Financial Aid.

Admission decisions will be mailed on March 10 if the admission process is completed by January 14. Please call the Admissions Office if you have any questions.

Application to be Completed by Parent

Full name of student _____   Nickname _____ ☐ Girl ☐ Boy

Applicant for grade _____ Age last birthday _____   Date of birth _____/_____/_____

Home address _____   Present school _____

City _____   Principal _____

Zip/Postal code _____   School address _____

Country of citizenship _____   City _____

Telephone (   ) _____   Zip/Postal code _____ Country _____

Telephone (   ) _____

Name of father _____   Name of mother _____

Occupation _____   Occupation _____

Position _____   Position _____

Employer _____   Employer _____

Business Address _____   Business Address _____

_____   _____

Telephone (   ) _____   Telephone (   ) _____

Has this child applied to our school before? ☐ Yes ☐ No   If yes, when? _____

Previous connection, if any, with our school: _____

_____

mother/father/sister/uncle/etc.

Other children in applicant's family:

Name	Birthdate	Gender	School	Grade
_____	___/___/	_____		
_____	___/___/	_____		
_____	___/___/	_____		

Are both parents living? ☐ Yes ☐ No   Are parents divorced? ☐ Yes ☐ No

Are parents separated? ☐ Yes ☐ No   If divorced, name of custodial parent: _____

Student lives with: _____

Please describe any personal characteristics, particular academic or extracurricular interests, or special circumstances of the applicant which you wish to bring to our attention.

A recent photograph would be helpful but is optional.

Please tell us why you are interested in our school for your child.

Please comment on any information or issues that may help give us a deeper understanding of your child's learning style.

Is the candidate an applicant for financial aid? _____

It is the family's responsibility to ensure that the candidate's folder is complete.

This application must be accompanied by a **$75.00 *nonrefundable* fee.** Please complete both sides of the application.

Date _____
Signature of parent or guardian responsible for financial obligations

Application to be Completed by Student

The candidate should complete this form in his or her own handwriting with no assistance.

Name _____   By what name do you like to be called? _____

Date of birth _____/_____/_____   Current school _____

Approximately how many books have you read during the past year, aside from required school texts? ____

Have you sung in a chorus or glee club? _____   How long? _____

Participated in dramatics? _____   In what capacity? _____

_____

Have you studied a musical instrument? ☐ Yes   ☐ No   Currently? _____

Which one and for how long? _____

On what athletic teams have you played? _____

How many years? _____   What positions? _____

_____

What other sports interests do you have? _____

_____

In what other organizations (school, religious, community, etc.) have you been an active participant?

_____

_____

Have you held an office? _____   When? _____

Position held? _____

What hobbies or other activities do you actively pursue? _____

_____

What have you done during the past two summers? (camp, travel, work, etc.)

_____

_____

_____

List any distinctions or honors you have won, academic or otherwise, in the last two years:

_____

_____

_____

Why are you interested in attending our school? _____

_____

_____

_____

_____

Please answer the following questions as clearly and concisely as you can.

1. Who is a person you admire and/or who has influenced you most? Why?

2. What currently interests you most (in or out of school?)

3. What else would you like to tell us about yourself?

4. On a separate sheet of paper, handwrite or type a 200–400 word essay on one of the following topics:

   a. Choose a character you admire from a book you have read and describe your thoughts and feelings about him or her.

   b. Write about an activity, place, or object that you love.

Signed _____

Date _____

Recommendation of Current Teachers

Parents, please forward directly to teacher after November 15.

Dear Colleague:

A student of yours, _____, grade _____, has applied to our school. In order to accurately assess this child's chances for success at our school, we would be grateful if you could complete the following recommendation form. The checklist format helps us evaluate areas of general interest, but we hope you will supplement this with your comments as well. This information will remain confidential in the Admissions Office. We thank you for taking the time to help us and the applicant.

Using a scale of 1–5, please rate the student in each of these areas.
1–superior   2–very good   3–average   4–below average   5–weak

Effort		Intellectual Potential		Concern for others	
Attitude		Motivation		Self-discipline	
Study Habits		Maturity		Peer relationships	
Intellectual curiosity		Class participation		Leadership potential	
Sense of humor		Extracurricular participation			

Please comment on any of your ratings and on any other characteristics of the student that you feel would help us understand him or her better. Use back or another sheet if necessary. **PLEASE DO NOT LEAVE BLANK.**

If you would like to discuss this candidate by phone, please check here. ☐

Print name _____   Telephone (   )

School _____   Subject

Address _____

Signature _____   Date

Please sign and return to the Admissions Office at the above address as soon after November 15 as possible.

Biography

Lila Lohr graduated from an independent school, studied political science at Vassar College, and earned an M.Ed. from Goucher College. Ms. Lohr worked as a teacher and administrator in several independent schools and was headmistress of St. Paul's School for Girls in Baltimore, Maryland. She is currently the Head of School at Princeton Day School, a JK–12 coed day school in Princeton, New Jersey. A parent of 3 private school graduates, Ms. Lohr has written extensively on education and parenting.

NOTES

NOTES